WOMEN'S INTUITION

Women's Intuition

Elizabeth Davis

Celestial Arts
Berkeley, California

CELESTIAL ARTS
P.O. Box 7327
Berkeley, California 94707

Cover design by Ken Scott
Cover art by TRIAD CLC
Text design by Nancy Austin
Composition by Wilsted & Taylor, Oakland
Set in Erhardt

Library of Congress Cataloging-in-Publication Data
Davis, Elizabeth, 1950–
    Women's intuition/Elizabeth Davis.
        p.   cm.
    Bibliography: p.
    Includes index.
    ISBN 0-89087-572-3
    1. Women—Psychology   2. —Intuition
    (Psychology)   I. Title.
HQ1206.D345   1989
155.6'33—dc20   89-31870
                                                    CIP

First Printing, 1989

1 3 5 7 9 0 8 6 4 2

Manufactured in the United States of America

To Carole

CONTENTS

ACKNOWLEDGMENTS

Acknowledgments on a work like this must necessarily be wide-ranging. I want first to thank my special women friends for the depth of intimacy from which this project springs. I thank also my clients and students, for allowing me to share their innermost growth processes. To *every* woman who, with a touch or glance, has acknowledged the core of who I am, my heartfelt appreciation.

A special acknowledgment to the Center for Applied Intuition (San Francisco) and John F. Kennedy University (Orinda, CA) for the milestone conference, "Opening the Intuitive Gate" (1988). To the many speakers who moved me profoundly—Anne and Jim Armstrong, Robert Gerard,

Helen Palmer and Angeles Arrien, to name a few—my gratitude for your research and wisdom.

Of course, without the excellent work of the Celestial Arts staff—Paul Reed, Dayna Macy, Maryann Anderson, Nancy Austin and my editor, David Hinds—this project would not have come to fruition. Thanks also to Mary Rose for moral support and word processing.

To my children and husband, a very special thanks for your part in all this.

And finally, to the midwives with whom I work and celebrate, an acknowledgment of the richness of your skills in the intuitive capacity.

—Elizabeth Davis
San Francisco, 1989

WOMEN'S INTUITION

CHAPTER I

What Is Intuition?

I remember the exact moment I first professed my interest in intuition. I had just given birth to my daughter at home, a great triumph after a difficult hospital delivery with the first. Both little ones were fast asleep, and my husband and I were sitting quietly in front of the fireplace with a dear friend of many years, who suddenly turned to me and asked in a way both knowing and genuinely curious, "So, Liz, what next?" I responded without thinking, surprising myself as I spoke, "Well, I really want to learn how to develop my intuition."

As it was, in the weeks that followed with my newborn I got something of a crash course! But now, many years later I reflect that my sense of intuitive capacity has in fact been borne out by my life, realized slowly over time. In my work as author and midwife, in the roles of wife, mother, counselor and friend, intuition has figured strongly in my approach to problem-solving and my search for deeper meaning, greater understanding. Although I definitely use rational abilities to gather information, I rely fully on my intuition to show me what to *do* with it.

Intuition for problem-solving—does this ring a bell for you? For many of us, the use of intuition is so incorporated in our daily lives that we may not recognize it as such. Or we may choose to call it by other, less controversial names like "common sense" or "insight." In the past, the term "women's intuition" has been synonymous with superstitious tale-telling, sensationalism or paranoia. But now, as women surmount many years of cultural handicap and become integrated and articulate, this term assumes new meaning. Don't you agree that in this day and age, with our seasoned sophistication and desire to move forward, women's intuition is a force to be reckoned with? Don't you feel that your own intuition is really quite powerful?

I imagine so, or you wouldn't be holding this book. Yet few of us have deliberately set out to develop intuition, figuring we either had it or we didn't—depending on the circumstances it might be "on" or "off" but was basically beyond control. Essentially, this is true. Intuitive function cannot be commanded, bought or manufactured. However, there do seem to be certain triggers of intuitive awareness, along with ways to recognize and validate it.

And yes, there are also ways to hone ourselves to be

more available to the workings of intuition. And that is what this book is all about.

A bit more personal history: it wasn't until I had practiced as a midwife for a number of years and had handled several life/death crises with a facility clearly exceeding my own knowledge base that I became fully convinced of the existence of intuition. I did some reading and queried my friends in an attempt to understand the basics. As I began to take midwifery students, I sought ways to incorporate intuitive training with clinical instruction, experimenting with self-awareness and emotional clearing techniques. Although the traditional medical model has little or no regard for intuition, many of my colleagues shared first-hand experience and a definite fascination with the subject. Those most familiar with intuition (or most willing to talk about it) have been women.

Why is this so? Women have certain cultural advantages when it comes to expressing their inner lives, and although intuition is distinct from emotion, it is certainly closer to it than to rational thought. In general, we are not expected to be as tough and calloused as men. And we have certain biological opportunities for developing intuition through childbearing and child rearing that cannot be denied.

More on this in Chapter Two; for now, I want to make it very clear that it is not my premise that women are necessarily more intuitive than men. *All* of us have intuition; as the experts in the field agree, it's part of the equipment. Nevertheless it is the feminine aspect, the receptive element that *plays the central role* in the intuitive process. My purpose

Qualities of Intuitive People

◆ Confident

◆ Independent, self-sufficient

◆ Unconventional

◆ Emotionally involved in abstract issues

◆ Willing and unafraid to explore
   uncertainties, entertain doubts

◆ Comfortable with criticism and challenge

◆ Able to accept criticism, or reject if
   necessary

◆ Willing to change

◆ Resistant to outside control and direction

◆ Foresighted

◆ Spontaneous

—from Malcolm Westcott's *Toward a Contemporary
   Psychology of Intuition*

for writing on this subject springs from my experience of working intimately with women and from my desire that we be empowered in our innate capacities. For too long we have been driven to emulate the masculine and have thus exacerbated the crisis of a culture out of balance.

But now, before we go any further, we need a working definition of intuition. Webster's is simple enough: "immediate apprehension or cognition, the power or faculty of attaining to direct knowledge without rational inference." Frances Vaughan, authority on the subject, describes intuition as "true by definition" and further states, "If a seemingly intuitive insight turns out to be wrong, it did not spring from intuition but from self-deception or wishful thinking." Prolific metaphysical author Alice Bailey calls intuition "apprehension of reality exactly as it is." And of the process itself, Angeles Arrien, expert on the subjects of tarot and women's mysteries, finds meaning in the very sound of the word, *in-tu-it*.

One way to clarify the meaning of intuition is to look at what it is not, i.e., logical, rational function. As you are no doubt aware, our society is based on the premise that there is only one reliable mode for acquiring information, and that is by deductive reasoning. The phenomenon of intuition is therefore unacknowledged, discredited or highly suspect. This lopsided view pervades our scientific methodology, our approach to medicine, education, business, personal relationships and daily interactions. In fact, one might well say that logic is our religion; we are taught that true knowledge resides outside ourselves, apart from any internal sense of knowing. Our society is utterly dualistic, in contrast to indigenous cultures where logic and intuition are united by a strong sense of connection to nature. We seek to control nature, dominate her and in so doing, sever ourselves from the instinctive awareness fundamental to intuitive function.

The rational mind is *finite*, it works on the basis of specific facts and information already stored and processed. Intuitive awareness, on the other hand, appears to be *infinite:* how else can we explain the occurrence of precognition, retrocognition, clairvoyance and telepathy?

As Margo Adair observes in her wonderful book, *Working Inside Out*, "We have a rich language to enable us to use our rational consciousness, but virtually no language for tapping the creative or insightful powers of innerconsciousness." Thus, most of us are able to recognize intuition only in retrospect. I can think of many a time I've been driving in the car and have had a sudden impulse to change my direction, even though my current route promises to be the most timesaving, enjoyable, etc. Generally, if I ignore the message, I'll find myself in either a traffic jam or near collision. Perhaps you've had the experience of suddenly not wanting to attend a meeting—not for fear or anxiety, but with a clear sense that it's best not to go. If you're anything like me, you then split yourself in two and stage a debate between your rational mind and intuitive voice; the former bringing up every possible reason why staying home might be foolish, paranoid, etc., while the latter quietly persists. Rational chatter can seldom negate an intuitive message completely but it certainly can cloud the picture, particularly if emotions also come into play!

Learning to tell the difference between thoughts, feeling and intuitions *is* difficult at first, but can become easy with practice. Here are several key ways to differentiate.

Our thoughts are generally complex, categorical and sequential. Our emotions have a definite charge attached: they are either stirring or disturbing. We may *react* to intuition with either, but intuitive messages are subtle, simple, they stand by themselves, uncluttered and unfettered. To quote Adair once more, "Ask yourself how or why you know what you know; if you *can't* answer then it's an intuition." Along the same lines, Anne Armstrong, a well-known psychic, teaches her students to recognize intuition by its pervasiveness: if in spite of all rationalization and emotional gymnastics a message persists, then it's probably genuine.

If this seems a little soft and subjective to you, don't fret; there is a more scientific way to approach the subject, via a basic understanding of brain function. In this age of high technology, most of us have had some exposure to the electroencephalogram, or EEG. This measures brain waves, which fall into four general classifications: beta, alpha, theta and delta. What is germane to our discussion here is that each of these correlates to a particular state of mind, or level of consciousness.

Beta waves are the fastest and are typical of rational, cause-and-effect thinking, goal-orientation and clock-time awareness. We emit a flurry of beta waves whenever we are in a hurry or are busy coordinating several activities simultaneously. Beta waves help us get by in a fast-paced world, they enable us to get organized by focusing on *particulars*.

Beta is appropriate for certain mental processes, but as a mode of being isolates and separates us from one another.

The "competitive edge" many of us feel compelled to maintain in various areas of our lives is really beta edginess, which if not tempered with the subtler energies of relatedness, can lead to tremendous stress and anxiety.

These subtler energies are found in the alpha state; alpha waves are slower and more synchronized than beta, and are characteristic of an internal (rather than external) focus. Any relaxing and fairly automatic activity can induce an alpha state, which is receptive and diffused, thus conducive to intuitive awareness (remember the example of my hunch while driving?) Rhythmic activities such as jogging, dancing, weaving and swimming are especially evocative. Meditation with awareness of one's breathing rhythm also triggers a shift to alpha.

Alpha is literally right below the surface. A classic example of the intuitive process is found in the story of the inventor who, having struggled with facts and figures until nearly exhausted, took a walk in the woods and paused to rest when "Eureka," the answer to her dilemma suddenly emerged. Usually this surprise solution is not so specific as encompassing, a sudden comprehension of overall pattern that brings all the pieces (so carefully assembled in beta) together. Similarly, when we stop trying to articulate all we know we often discover the *context* for our information.

It makes sense that if concentration has been intense in a particular area and is abruptly released, regrouping and cohesion can occur "out of the blue." On the other hand, glimpses of the larger picture may emerge without any prefocusing, e.g., knowledge of traffic safety patterns in an area we're approaching or awareness of social patterns at a party we suddenly feel we'd rather not attend. The key is letting go, getting "out of our heads."

Theta waves are decidedly slower than alpha, and as such do not figure very strongly in our day-to-day lives. Keep in mind that *as brain waves slow, they become more synchronous*—whereas in ordinary consciousness we have a mixture of beta, alpha, theta and delta, in a theta state the higher frequencies are largely absent. Thus theta consciousness is *one-pointed*, creating a sense of union with all existence, i.e., mystical or transcendent awareness.

Theta is completely receptive, so much so that one is only aware of what is happening in the moment, without any thought of what might happen next. There is no weighing and considering alternatives as in the beta state, in fact, there is no considering at all, *just being*. In an alpha state we are still conscious of space, time, where and what we are, but in theta we merge with our experience and these distinctions fall away.

Deep hypnosis can induce this state, so may tantric (or otherwise ecstatic) lovemaking. Psychedelic drugs tend to concentrate brain waves in theta frequency; likewise any life-threatening struggle for survival. As those with some first-hand experience agree, all attention is focused on the moment, concentrated on the immediate situation. One feels funnelled inward and yet oddly expanded, extremely open and yet locked into the bigger picture. Those who return from the edge of death often report that their lives passed before them—this is *total revelation of pattern* (barely perceivable in the alpha state) that stands altogether outside time.

Kathlyn Rhea, author of *Mind Sense*, maintains that high adrenaline levels are key to intuitive function. Certainly this is relevant to near-death/survival situations, but there are several considerations. Adrenaline actually speeds up brain waves and puts us firmly in a beta state. How then do we make the abrupt transition to theta? Perhaps in the event of overload, we literally burn out and drop instinctively to survival level. Adrenaline is also involved in sexual excitation, which with extreme passion, sacred intention or exalted love may shift us through alpha and down to theta.

Remember what was said earlier about learning to disregard intuition, via cultural messages? Adair believes that children reside in theta much of the time up until the age of two. If you are a mother who has marveled at her little one's frequent precognitions, or have likewise been frustrated by your toddler's inability to grasp time frames or the notion of consequence, now you have an explanation!

The exact reason why theta waves open a window to expanded consciousness (and the most profound forms of intuition) is not yet clear. Numerous intuitives, theologians and even "hard" scientists agree that there must be an energy field or plane in which the usual distinctions of time and space cease to exist. Some refer to this as the causal plane, some the fifth dimension—whatever the terminology, it appears that here is a realm of being wherein all that has been, is, and will be *exists simultaneously*. In other words, this repository of past and future information encompasses our usual reality.

Granted, this is metaphysical and somewhat vague, but

there is more. Let's look at some major discoveries in the realm of physics.

In attempting to break down the atom to identify the most basic building blocks or units of materiality, scientists were puzzled and amazed to find a reality that defied the usual concepts of space/time. The most minute unit of matter turned up as both wave and particle—not a particle *on* a wave, *but both at once!*[1] Now, how can anything be stationary and moving, solid and diffused all at the same time? Clearly, at the very core of our being, on a subatomic level, time is just an illusion, a condition of state.

So it seems, nearly anything is possible. Theta waves take us to these deep, basic levels of consciousness where we can experience this extraordinary reality, bits and pieces of which return with us as intuitive knowledge when we rise to the surface again.

Perhaps you know something of the split-brain theory, and are wondering how this connects. In general, it has been established that the left hemisphere tends to deal with rapid, sequential changes, analyzing data in terms of specifics, while the right hemisphere deals with abstract relationships and patterns. At first glance it might appear that the left brain is responsible for beta function, the right for alpha. However, research has shown sharp functional division only in subjects whose brains were literally split or damaged, either by injury or surgery for tumors, epilepsy, etc.[2] In the normal, healthy brain, similarity and replication of function between hemispheres is much more common.

Besides, I think it important to remember that this

theory deals only with the cerebral cortex and leaves out other parts of the brain. The limbic system, for example, is known to be the seat of emotional function and is considered responsible for certain primitive responses of survival. Surely it is somehow involved in intuition engendered by ecstatic or crisis situations. Psychiatrist/philosopher Eugene d'Aquili has speculated that the highly aroused limbic system may have the ability to *unify* both hemispheres, so that the brain is flushed free of dichotomy. Indeed, biofeedback findings on those in deeply meditative states confirm that interhemispheric coherence is highest in transcendent states.[3]

All of which brings us back to what was said earlier about brain wave coherence in theta. As Phillip Goldberg, author of *The Intuitive Edge* observes, "at the deepest level our mind has more in common with others; it is less individuated." Beta waves are the most cortical of our vibrations, and the most certain to create static interference with the underlying and universal patterns of theta.

So why the cultural skepticism regarding something so obviously valid and real? Of all the studies of intuition, *not one* has been made with participants in the altered states most conducive to intuitive function. Adrenaline as a factor has yet to be acknowledged, let alone utilized as a stimulus. No wonder we're told there is no scientific evidence to support the existence of the paranormal, despite the fact that personal experiences abound. As far as I'm concerned there is *no question* as to whether or not intuition exists; it's as much a part of us as anything else.

Those in touch with their intuitive abilities report tremendous feelings of integration and purpose. In both alpha and theta states, we experience alignment of body, mind and spirit, contributing to optimal health. As Shakti Gawain says in her fine book, *Living in the Light*, "By learning to contact, listen to and act on our intuition, we can directly connect to the higher power of the universe and allow it to become our guiding force." The urge to understand and tap intuition is a *positive* one, a healthy, natural desire.

In Chapter Three, "Making Friends with Your Intuitive Voice," we will look more closely at ways to develop intuition. But first, let's explore the unique capacities of ourselves as women in this regard.

---

1. Capra, Fritjof, *The Tao of Physics* (Berkeley, CA: Shambhala, 1975).

2. Springer, Sally and Deutsch, George, *Left Brain, Right Brain* (San Francisco: W. H. Freeman, 1981).

3. d'Aquili, Eugene G., "The Neurobiological Basis of Myth and Concepts of Deity," *Zygon* (1978).

CHAPTER 2

*Women &
the Intuitive Process*

We know that intuition is a natural function, and that all of us have inherent intuitive abilities. Why then has intuition so long been considered the province of women? Cultural factors are obviously at play, and we'll look at these in a moment. But what of biological factors? Are there differences between the sexes (hormonally induced, perhaps) that influence intuitive ability?

I think so, and what little research there has been in this area tends to concur. With regard to problem-solving in general, men are more narrowly focused and concerned with specifics while women are more sensitive to context, more receptive to subliminal and peripheral information—the stuff of which intuition is made. Male orientation to the tangible has been shown to *begin in infancy*, i.e., it does not appear to be culturally induced.[1]

In terms of actual brain function, women appear more able to switch from one side to another. Considering the link between interhemispheric coherence and high-level intuition, this certainly seems significant. However, it can also be argued that patterns of hemispheric usage are socially induced.

And how might a woman's intuitive development be socially affected? On the one hand she is apt to be indulged for her feelings, granted emotional liberties definitely denied men. She is likely to be excused when overcome, shocked or grieved, permitted integrity of being in many instances. However, there are other emotions she is expected to censor such as anger, rage or open defiance.

Until fairly recently, women in our culture have been barred from business, politics, worldly interactions. This is in contrast to the matriarchies of yore, by far the dominant social structure since human inception. In these, women were honored as leaders, revered for their natural abilities to create life and express the mysteries of existence. Although our history books refer to these early societies as primitive, archaeological and anthropological findings reveal that many were highly advanced, both technologically and culturally. They were egalitarian, with few of the social imbalances and ills that plague today's world. Also remarkable were a lack of weaponry and of the trappings of centralized religion; these were cultures of peace, with shrines and altars everywhere.[2]

How we ended up where we are today is another story.

For now, consider the impact of living in a society that defines women as second-class by denying such basic rights as equal pay for equal services, equal social security benefits, etc. Under the pretense of reverence and protection, our culture has undermined women's autonomy, common-sense wisdom and natural leadership. While struggling to be self-reliant in both inner and outer worlds, women have all the while been forced to maintain their own pretense of passivity. The times may be changing, but progress is slow, and in the meantime women experience their knowingness largely in secret, or in the relative security of one another's company. Even those in positions of power often find they must keep their knowledge carefully veiled.

One fringe benefit of playing the passive role has been the cultivation of incredible patience and forbearance. These qualities are critical when it comes to nurturing life, but blend with assertive self-expression in more balanced societies. As *passive* nurturers, women must find ways of getting what they want or feel is necessary without speaking out directly. Women are known to be good judges of others; perhaps they have *had* to be in order to avoid false moves or missteps that would have resulted in punishment or ridicule. On a practical level, they've *needed* to know when a family member was either physically or emotionally unstable, lest the household fall apart and the blame fall on their shoulders.

As women have entered the work force in recent years, they have had to deal with these same culturally-induced role expectations (make the coffee, interpret and soothe the boss's moods and generally keep quiet) if wanting to advance. Self-defense and open confrontation are more acceptable than before, but for many, many years, women were *silent survivors*, and as such used their intuition to read between the lines, interpret non-verbal cues and recognize patterns of probability in order to plan their next moves.

Beyond a doubt, our society is deeply alienated from the feminine aspect and its power. Many of us have been frightened of it ourselves, and have tried to divorce this irrational and spontaneous element from the rest of our lives, only to have it rise up unexpectedly in daily doings or else emerge vividly in dreams. According to Western religious doctrine, this "dark" side of human nature must be controlled, subdued by reason. But the key to a full and happy life lies in integrating the two, forging a union of male and female aspects that honors and maintains the integrity of each. This is also essential for accessing and utilizing intuition!

In their excellent book, *Women's Ways of Knowing*, authors Belenky, Clinchy, Goldberg and Tarule present results of a study indicating several major stages through which women pass in the development of self, voice and mind.[3] The great value of their system is that it not only shows that an integrated state is conducive to intuition, but chronicles the tremendous effort, the struggles through doubt and confusion necessary to reach that state. As we examine these stages one by one, I'm sure you'll find yourself "remembering when" as I did on my first reading!

STAGE ONE: SILENCE
This is a state of feeling disconnected from one's own thoughts, voice, power. At this stage, women believe only in external authorities and have no confidence in their own experience.

STAGE TWO: RECEIVED KNOWING
At this stage, a woman obtains identity through conforming to others' expectations; she becomes a "good girl," "good student," and "good wife" or "good employee." Sense of authority arises by identifying with a group's power or beliefs.

STAGE THREE: SUBJECTIVE KNOWING
This is the stage when a woman becomes self-aware and connects with her inner voice for the first time. This often means turning away from others, denial of external authority as truth becomes a personal, private matter. However this is still a dualistic state, the "right" information being on the inside, the "wrong" on the outside.

STAGE FOUR: PROCEDURAL KNOWING
This stage is often one of difficulty and disillusionment, wherein a woman's knowledge is declared either incomplete or inaccurate by some outside authority. In order to address this challenge she must find external reference points, ways to express the *reasons* for her beliefs and/or actions. This may mean a temporary loss of contact with, or faith in, her inner voice.

STAGE FIVE: CONSTRUCTED KNOWING
This stage marks the attempt to integrate knowledge felt subjectively with what has been learned through others. This is accomplished by thinking *inclusively*, rather than

dualistically. Women now incorporate themselves in the acquisition of knowledge or, as one study subject stated succinctly, "you let the inside out, and the outside in."

Although these stages are more or less sequential, one may be at an advanced stage overall while lagging behind in a particular respect. And too, there is much individual variation on how much time is spent backtracking before the move to the next stage is finally complete. For the purposes of our discussion, let's begin with a closer look at stage three.

Although the authors considered this subjective phase to be intuitive, it seems to me more likely to produce superstition, fanaticism or at best, intuition without context. Without the complement of rational input and review, something is missing. Nevertheless, of the 135 women in this study (representing a complete spectrum of age, class, educational and ethnic backgrounds) over 50% were found to be in this stage.

One of the main things these women had in common was the experience of *failed male authority*. For some this occurred in an academic setting, for others, interpersonally or with regard to family members. Typically, a female friend, mother, grandmother or social worker is substituted during the transition from outer to inner authority.

Women reach stage four when they choose to respond to the challenge of the outside world again, though many at first want only to flee or return to inner sanctum. What tips the scales is the determination that the cost of escape is somehow too great, involving sacrifice of career goals, loss of a major relationship, etc. It helps tremendously if the challenger is less an adversary than a mentor, "neither vicious nor absent." With a sense of support, a woman will more readily learn to substantiate her positions.

Nevertheless this can be a very lonely time, a time when it seems that spirit and intuition have died away completely, a time when one fears for the loss of one's soul. What saves a lot of women at this juncture is the discovery of what the authors called *connected knowing*, i.e., working out rationale and logical defense in a *group* situation. By participating in professional organizations, women's studies classes or self-help/support groups, women learn by empathy, sharing their "half-baked truths" in a nurturing environment. Through a process of collaboration, they begin to measure personal knowledge against the authority of others.

By the time women reach stage five they have integrated the voices of inner and outer; they are complete. How can such a major shift occur? Women at this crossroads often *take time off somehow*, removing themselves psychologically or even geographically from all they have known and been. They speak of searching for the pattern of their selves, moving beyond the given. In some ways this is reminiscent of the subjective phase; only then the inner voice was so new that all outer voices had to be ignored. Now either/or thinking is abandoned, as a woman realizes that thought is constructed of many parts and *it is she* who plays the central role. Whereas subjective women tend to oversimplify issues and procedurally-oriented women are threatened by conflict, constructivists see disagreement as an invitation to growth, complexity as ground for distillation.

Stage five is one of *passionate* knowing. Women enter

into a union with what they wish to understand. As you may recall, merging with the subject at hand is also characteristic of a high-level intuitive state.

If this overview feels somewhat overwhelming, just take what you can from it and keep in mind that all systems must be adapted to suit the situation. And do not think that intuition is only possible at stage five; remember, it's part of the equipment. What we *can* learn from this system is the best possible psychological context for *accessing, interpreting* and *expressing* intuition. The more integrated we are, the greater our self-knowledge and love, the more likely we'll be able to do all three.

I don't know about you, but when I read through these stages the first time I felt as though someone had finally articulated and given meaning to the course of my life. Events that had heretofore seemed either random, insignificant or unfortunate suddenly became important, respectable. I remembered myself as a child, and the terrible trouble I had at school when I innocently used inner authority to answer questions and ended up sounding smug or conceited. All the while I was growing up, the schism between the "real world" and my inner life intensified until I reached a crisis point in college. It seemed that all my professors (most of them men) wanted me to put aside personal feelings for the sake of rational discourse, until my academic prostitution was so complete that I routinely cranked out the "perfect paper" without any feeling of relationship to what I was saying. When I finally left school, I did so in order to find myself.

Disappointments in love only intensified my confusion. Despite all conditioning to the contrary, I found that men did not have the answers I was looking for. I learned that relationship was not just magical chemistry, but sprang from my ability to love and trust myself. I then began sharing with women in groups, first in the context of communal living and later in my work as a childbirth educator and midwifery student. It was there that I found my greatest support, and the courage to blend hard facts with my most intimate thoughts and feelings.

When I eventually became a midwife, I faced the challenges of a hostile medical profession and dubious public. Finding ways to substantiate my beliefs and intuitions regarding my work was both stimulating and terrifying, but the end result was a merger of selves, a sense of my own destiny plus the energy to carry out my dreams.

To return to the theme touched on earlier, what this process is really about is the alignment of masculine and feminine energies within us. Because it serves to connect us to the universal, the proper role of feminine energy should be to *guide and inform* our actions. Action itself, as an expression of our inner vision, is appropriate use of masculine energy. In other words, male energy (in either sex) should respond in *all-out service* to the wisdom of the feminine side.

But once again we are culturally opposite, using male energy to *suppress and control* the female. In the traditional role, a woman forces down and denies her feminine power, her intuition. This leaves her "helpless, dependent on men, emotionally unbalanced and able to express her power only through manipulation."[4] If, on the other hand, a woman has her inner voice in the driver's seat and puts her male energy in action to back it up—well, just imagine!

In her work on this subject, Gawain shares a memorable image that came to her in meditation. She envisioned her feminine side as a "beautiful, radiant queen, overflowing with love and light," riding through streets on a litter and healing those gathered near by way of her openness and compassion. Her male aspect appeared as a samurai warrior carrying a sword, walking at the queen's side ever ready to defend her should anyone make a threatening move. A clear and lovely vision of male and female energies in healthy relationship!

To return to the question raised earlier about whether or not women have any biological advantage when it comes to intuitive function, there is more to consider. It is my opinion that women are blessed with certain physiologic occurrences which serve to express and reiterate this healthy balance of power. But due to our conditioning we're hard-pressed to appreciate these, let alone see them as opportunities for intuitive growth. Take for example the monthly (or thereabouts) event of menstruation. It occurs at a point when both estrogen and progesterone levels drop off, a natural ebb in the flow. It gives us a "breather," a break in our outwardly-focused routine through which we can relax and regroup. Many women use this time for not only physical but emotional release, a chance to let themselves weep, be irrational and reflective, plumb the emotional depths and get fully in touch with their true feelings. This makes for a fresh start with the next cycle—a cleansed perspective with which to ride the wave of hormonal effects to the peak of ovulation and back again.

Menstruation is still considered by some to be a

"curse," largely because our culture finds functions of elimination embarrassing and maintains that the body is inferior to mind and spirit, or at best, separate. *But how can a woman separate the two when through her body she brings forth life, intelligent and aware?* She is tied by her monthly cycle to lunar influences; both menstruation and ovulation tend to coincide with either full or new moon. Thus she is automatically part of a bigger picture, linked to that beyond herself.

And how does Premenstrual Syndrome (PMS) fit into all this? Apart from severe cases due to hormonal imbalances or dietary deficiencies, I think PMS is more likely to occur whenever we are unwilling or unable to "let our hair down" and take stock of ourselves. We have more control over our cycles than we think: at one point I managed to shift from a twenty-eight day cycle with a full week of unpleasant symptoms to a twenty-one day cycle that was nearly trouble-free, simply by facing some emotional issues I'd been neglecting. Another time I was troubled with extremely intense feelings and heavy bleeding as my periods came regularly on the full moon and I thought to myself, "Wouldn't it be better to menstruate on the new moon, and ovulate on the full? I think I'll work on that." Sure enough, within several months my cycle had shifted around completely! It is also significant that women who work together or are very close tend, over time, to synchronize their cycles, menstruating and ovulating in harmony.

In the context of providing women's health care, I am often asked what I think of the Pill. Although most women worry about physical side-effects, few have ever considered the psychological aspects. The truth is that the Pill robs a woman of her natural cycle, of the peaks and valleys that reflect her state of being, putting her instead on automatic pilot, always the same, hormonally monotone. Even the sequential formula, which alternates progesterone and estrogen in a way designed to replicate the natural cycle, still dictates a fixed and foreign pattern. We've already considered the function of menstruation, the lessons of ebb, but have not yet looked at the joys and richness of the ovulation phase. How empowering it was for me to learn fertility awareness, to observe the sweet and intense desire I had when fertile and to own it at last, no longer under the illusion that it was caused or created by any man! Many women dream profoundly when ovulating, dreams of birth, creation and desire that are most revealing to them personally. Although the Pill is right for some, and certainly provides security in terms of contraception, loss of one's natural rhythms and interrelatedness is quite a price to pay!

It's also worth mentioning that when a woman has been on the Pill for some time and then decides to quit, she may not ovulate or menstruate for months—the body forgets what to do and needs time to reorganize. In this transitional phase, emotional ups and downs are like never before as hormone levels shift and sway, struggling to stabilize. A very intense and *condensed* period of making up for lost time and awareness, it would seem!

Attunement to the monthly cycle is small potatoes, though, to the tremendous growth and learning opportunities of pregnancy and birth. In fact, looking back on the developmental phases outlined earlier, birth is often the cat-

alyst for moving beyond the duality of subjective and procedural knowing; even a woman lost in silence may find her
voice for the first time. This is largely due to the unifying
effect of pregnancy; both spiritual and physical awareness
intensify and are inextricably blended.

A pregnant woman is typically absent-minded and for-
getful, due to circulatory changes and the overall slowing of
her metabolism. The fringe benefit, however, is that she is
much more likely to slip into alpha states on a routine basis.
Also, she is in the utterly paradoxical and therefore trans-
formative condition of literally being two people at once,
enough to kick in theta awareness through sheer resonance.
Pregnant women are *very* intuitive (although they are also
more vulnerable to fear and anxiety, obstacles we'll consider
in Chapter Three.)

I recall a close friend asking during my last pregnancy
what sex I thought my baby was. I gave her everyone else's
hunches, feelings, dreams, etc. (all "girl") but she insisted,
"No, besides all that, what do *you* think it is?" I answered immediately, "I think it's a boy." I've known with each of my
pregnancies, and after all, why not? Surely with a baby inside
you, your energy fields merged, part of you must *definitely*
know its sex (not to mention many other deep and intimate
truths about its nature!).

Whatever pregnancy may do to enhance intuitive ability, giving birth can do tenfold. In preparing women for
labor, I make it a point to explain that although books
and classes generally put the emphasis on technique, in fact
it's all in the moment, a matter of letting one's physical

intelligence respond to the overwhelming energy of the process. In short, they don't "do" birth, birth "does" them, and the key to gaining control is often to lose it, to surrender ideas, desires, fantasies and fears in order to merge with the experience. One has only to speak to women who have succeeded in giving birth this way to appreciate the power and glory possible with delivery!

Hormone levels rise and fall dramatically in the last weeks of pregnancy, causing women to be intensely aware of their feelings and needs moment-to-moment. Nesting instinct is fairly universal and usually manifests as fussing around the house, cleaning and straightening until finally settling in. As labor commences, women become so sensitized that they are able to read the thoughts and feelings of those around them with very little trouble. Later, once labor is well underway, many marvel to find themselves moving, breathing and taking positions with total spontaneity. This is beautiful to witness, the laboring woman completely vulnerable and yet fully in charge of her experience.

Although I don't believe that anyone has ever checked the brain waves of laboring women, I suspect that in this state of merger they are primarily theta. Attendants often speak of the "incredible energy in the room" and of feeling "drawn into the process." It's as though the birthing woman opens a window on the universal field for others to look through, whence comes the soul of her baby.

It is *especially* critical that a woman be open (and supported as such) in the event of difficult or prolonged labor, fully empowered by her attendants to intuit what will best help her relax and let go. Even in outright emergencies, maternal instinct tends to come through loud and clear as long as it is not censored.

In recent years women have insisted on the right to give birth actively (as opposed to lying back passively, drugged or restrained) which raises an interesting point. When a woman *delivers herself* of her child she is simultaneously in *fully receptive* and *fully expressive* modes. No wonder birth is, for many, a peak experience unequaled by any other! I have always found it remarkable that whenever I tell a woman I've just met that I'm a midwife, be she twenty-four or sixty-four years old, I'll likely be treated to a most personal and vivid account of her delivery, from the moment of the first contraction. Women *never forget* the experience of giving birth; it is a turning point, a revelation, and if it is disrupted or co-opted by attendants or technology, the results to self-esteem can be devastating. Then again, if a woman feels successful at giving birth she will often be catapulted to new levels of self-confidence and creative expression.

The Native American tradition (which holds the female in highest regard) teaches that the Creator gave women the ability to understand life's meaning through the intensity and pain of birth. Men, on the other hand, learn only through circumstantial suffering. Thus ceremonies are created specifically for them, utilizing stress or self-inflicted injury to approximate the purification that birthing brings naturally to women.[5]

Just how intense *is* the physical pain of labor? This varies greatly from woman to woman and depends on many factors. Ultimately the way of birth is highly personal, and nearly always involves some learning on the spot. Emotional pain and/or mental anguish may also be felt in breaking down barriers so the forces of labor can work unhindered. Giving birth is definitely an act of courage!

Life with a new baby is a remarkable time of non-verbal and highly intuitive communication. It is said that the hormone prolactin, released in breast milk, tends to synchronize maternal-infant sleep cycles. Thus a mother may wake moments before her baby, or they may wake together. It is further suggested that the prolactin link may foster a sort of telepathy between them wherein baby may wake and cry if mother has had a bad dream, or mother may sense her baby's needs precisely as they occur. This telepathic connection definitely lingers and may last a lifetime; I remember my little ones amazing me as they spoke my thoughts without any apparent stimulus, and now that they are teens, I usually know what's going on with them whether they tell me or not!

If you are still as yet contemplating motherhood and wondering if you'll ever be ready, consider this: many women make the mistake of examining the issue from a strictly rational point of view. Taking into account what's been said so far, the experience of becoming a parent simply cannot be circumscribed this way. Pregnancy and birth are *major life transitions*; as such, they are fraught with the difficulties of rapid growth that tend to *revolutionize* one's thinking and being. Even when I was pregnant with my third child (more or less planned and very much desired) I still experienced a good bit of fear in the beginning, not so much in terms of my ability to parent but for the monumental changes about to take place in me personally.

On the other hand, until you've had a child of your own

you can scarcely imagine the reassurance and fascination of hereditary linkage, or the astounding phenomenon that is maternal, instinctive love. As author Diane Mariechild says:

> In my life the physical acts of birthing, lactating and mothering have been an incredible means of sourcing my power. While these are not choices every woman would make, or should make, they are ones which have had an enormous impact on every aspect of my life. The joys and sorrows of motherhood have provided me with a wealth of knowledge and resources. It is my path of power and my spiritual practice.[6]

Mothering teaches us to listen well, receive the knowledge of our children and accept the chaos and conflict of growth as natural and necessary. By allowing a child's nature to distill itself through full self-expression, good mothering dissolves duality. Experienced mothers know very well that what works for their child one day may not work the next, and so rely increasingly (albeit unconsciously) on intuition to guide them. As the child grows, so can the mother!

What this boils down to is a philosophy of *empowering others to be their own authorities*. Women who have discovered how well this works in their families often extend this approach to professional relationships too, making their efforts in the business world remarkably efficient and successful. In their study, Belenky *et al.* found two distinct ways of handling authority: the "banker" approach, whereby duties, information and power are doled out from above; and the "midwife" approach, whereby the natural enthusiasm and talents of others are used to get things done. Feminine preference for the latter links powerfully to intuitive function. By supporting and aligning themselves with those around them, women in all walks of life discover an interrelatedness through which they intuit their appropriate role or position accurately and directly.

Adrienne Rich has said that of all things, "A woman needs to know she is capable of intelligent thought, and she needs to know it right away."[7] I would add that she also needs appropriate tools to assist her in exploring the full scope of her intelligence. In the next chapter we will look at some of the most powerful of these, and consider how each contributes to intuitive awakening.

1. Goldberg, Phillip, *The Intuitive Edge* (Los Angeles: Jeremy P. Tarcher, 1983).

2. Stone, Merlin, *When God Was a Woman* (New York: The Dial Press, 1976).

3. Belenky, Clinchy, Goldberg, Tarule, *Women's Ways of Knowing* (New York: Basic Books, Inc., 1986).

4. Gawain, Shakti, *Living in the Light* (San Rafael, CA: Whatever Publishing, 1986).

5. Ramirez, Larry, notes from panel, "What Is Intuition?" (San Francisco, 1988).

6. Mariechild, Diane, *The Inner Dance* (Freedom, CA: Crossing Press, 1987).

7. Rich, Adrienne, *On Lies, Secrets, and Silence: Selected Prose—1966-78* (New York: Norton, 1979).

CHAPTER 3

Making Friends with Your Intuitive Voice

Perhaps it has already dawned on you that the keys to enhancing intuition come from within, rather than "out of the blue." Although peak experiences may serve as triggers, awakening your intuitive ability in any lasting sense depends on increased self-awareness, the process of becoming whole.

We've seen already that at the height of the intuitive moment, one is aligned with universal energies. Ways to cultivate this alignment involve bringing body, conscious mind and spirit together. Or, as women in the constructivist phase of knowing found critical to a sense of well-being, "becoming and staying aware of the workings of their minds . . .

making the unconscious conscious . . . voicing the unsaid . . . consulting and listening to the self . . . staying alert to all the currents and undercurrents of life about them . . . weaving their passions and intellectual life into some recognizable whole."[1]

Let's break this down into basic areas of preparation. The first is learning to relax mind and body with some sort of *meditative activity*, the second, developing a flexible, non-judgmental attitude through *emotional clearing*, and the third, finding focus in life by developing integrity, or *authenticity*.

Another way to frame these would be:

1) letting go, loving yourself in relation to the universal;

2) examining fears and emotional projections, learning detachment;

3) bringing core energy, that which you truly are, into all areas of your life.

A tall order, indeed! But don't think you must master any or all of these in order to be intuitive. Developing intuition is a long-term project; it will take time to become aware and adept in each of these areas. Discovering and shifting around your own magical blend of techniques can and should be a lifetime joy and pleasure.

Meditation Redefined

I like Kathlyn Rhea's definition of meditation as "relaxing the senses." Unfortunately, both the purpose and practice of meditation have been largely misunderstood. If you've ever tried to meditate but quit because the stress of trying to control your wandering mind and wriggling body was just too much, don't despair. Any technique that calls for close concentration on a particular object or thought (mantra, holy concept, etc.) is more likely to *prevent* than induce expanded consciousness. The other extreme of trying to blank out all thought tends also to keep the mind from shifting to deeper levels where it can synchronize with the universal.

It is important to realize that most meditation systems have been designed by, and for, men. Considering their highly analytical propensities and aforementioned "orientation to tangible objects," it makes sense that men's meditation techniques might well involve subduing the body and stilling the mind. But how necessary and/or appropriate are such for women?

A major problem with these techniques is that they spring from and thus tend to support dualistic, mind-body belief systems for which women have little use or sympathy. And when it comes to self-control, women are more likely to have too much than too little, to the point of self-suppression. No, meditations for women should, in the words of Ms. Inglehart, help us "enliven and enjoy our

35

bodies . . . be active, love ourselves and develop and use the full power of our inner strength."

I like to think of meditation as anything we do that leads to a focused and integrated state of being. I meditate frequently by listening to music, bringing my physical, emotional and intellectual faculties together. I let go completely and become immersed, then find myself expanding to a highly cognizant, sensually satisfying state. One can also meditate while working on a puzzle or problem of some sort, while writing, or through physical activities like dancing and running (remember the alpha connection). Just letting ourselves "drift into reverie," for which we're often teased or reprimanded, is one of the most integrative meditative experiences.

Unlike ascetic forms of meditation where emotions are taboo, these activities *harness* the emotional energy of genuine enthusiasm (as psychic Anne Armstrong says, "You have to have a charge to make it work"). At the same time, the body is at ease because it's where it wants to be, and the mind is fully alert. Now *this* is meditation—effortless and natural!

This revised view links closely to the "passionate knowing" style of women who have integrated themselves. As you recall, they become consumed in the act of learning, merging with whatever they wish to understand. They are not afraid to stretch boundaries, or change them if necessary.[2] This ties to yet another way of entering an intuitive state, i.e., through deep appreciation, prayer, thankfulness, conscious love.

Now let me share with you a meditation technique that I've found quite special. This is a favorite of mine, something I've been doing for years but have only recently found reference to in several books as the practice of "running energy." Much like it sounds, the idea is to open up and let as much energy run through you as possible.

If you feel delightfully surprised by this notion, it's probably because you've found the opposite approach of controlled selectivity to be more draining than anything else. Yet this exercise has its own discipline, as you will see. I've found it to be particularly useful in my work as a midwife when I must stay alert for long hours into the night, or for aid in any stressful situation.

Running Energy

In a comfortable place and position, relax and
let your body go. Close your eyes, and be aware
of the energy inside you—does it feel a bit con-
fined, boxed-in? Let it begin to move now,
coursing through like your blood, your breathing. This should feel pleasant—warm and
tingling.

And what is the source? Feel the energy in
the space around you, and let the boundaries of
your body soften and dissolve. Open your eyes,
and feel how connected you are to everything
around you—it's all energy. Run it through,
and take in more if you'd like.

Now close your eyes once again and feel
this energy as boundless, ever-changing, ever-
moving yet somehow steady and reliable. Stay
with this as long as you like, open your eyes
when you're ready, and feel refreshed and
wonderful!

You can run energy any time—when alone or in the
midst of other activities. Try it at work, while making dinner,
when speaking to friends or associates (you can modify and
do it with your eyes open). You'll rarely ever be drained or
exhausted if you use this technique, because it keeps you
from getting snagged on anxieties, fears, desires, projections, etc. In effect, it replicates the spontaneous integration
we experience when fully at ease—the meditative state at
your fingertips!

The implications of this practice reach further still, particularly for anyone in the healing or helping professions.
When I first started practicing midwifery I believed it was
my job, my mission even, to give of myself to every client.
Consequently I would give *my* energy, rather than just energy! No wonder I burned out so quickly; I had to undergo
a major shift in attitude before being able to continue my
work. Thereafter, whenever the need arose, running energy
made me aware of the more transcendent aspects of chal-
lenging situations.

Now, for a change of pace, try this classic contemplation.

Time/Space

Think about a long time . . . an even longer
time . . . now double it . . . think of an even
longer period of time . . . longer still . . . now
think about eternity . . .[3]

I remember being about nine or ten and contemplating
such things at night in bed. Sometimes I would picture myself moving way out into space, until stopping at some point
I'd feel the boundlessness in every direction, going on for-
ever. Far from being frightening, this gave me an immense
feeling of excitement and belonging, as though I'd discovered the truth of my existence. When we let our minds wan-
der where our spirits lead, we are meditating in the truest
sense.

Emotional Clearing

According to Frances Vaughan, a "non-interfering alert
awareness, maintained in the midst of the inner world of
sensations, emotions and ideas, is the key to expanding intuition." This means learning to notice our feelings without
trying to do anything with or about them. But instead, we've
been taught to respond immediately, e.g., repress or ratio-
nalize upsetting feelings, glorify and prolong pleasing ones.

(Note how the advertising industry exploits and perpetuates the latter, and that the former is mandatory in the work-a-day world.) There is nothing *wrong* with feelings in and of themselves; in fact, they are sometimes vehicles for intuitive messages. It is our *attachment* to them that can break our connection to the overview and so disrupt intuitive awareness.

NOTICING FEELINGS

The first step in emotional clearing is learning to observe feelings for what they are. One simple way to do this is by keeping a journal of emotions, jotting them down periodically as they arise for perhaps a few hours each day. You'll soon see that the emotional fabric of your life is surprisingly complex—there are the big feelings that jump out at you, and the more subtle stream of responses that is almost continuous. Here is a particularly good exercise for dealing with upsetting or disturbing feelings.

> Bring one such feeling to the surface, and instead of reacting to it as you usually do, just sit with it, observe it. Then notice *where* you feel it physically, i.e., in what part of your body it seems focused. Perhaps you feel it all over—just see where it takes you.
>
> Now let yourself feel it as fully as possible. Go deeper into it, even further inside. What is at the *core* of your feeling? What is at its heart?

Basically, this teaches us to *disidentify* with our feelings. We can do this without turning off or shutting down, in fact, feeling emotions *all the way through* is the only way to transform them! As stated earlier, feelings are neither good nor bad, but they do provide up-to-the-minute information on our true state of being.

They also provide the means to connect intimately with others. Women in the constructivist phase reported a quantum increase in "empathetic potential,"[4] or what author Sara Ruddick refers to, interestingly enough, as "maternal thinking."[5] This ability to be fully sensitized to the internal lives of others develops only by becoming completely aware of our *own* inner workings. To do so is critical for yet another reason: if we are not fully aware of our feelings and able to set them aside when we choose, we may unconsciously project them into situations or onto others, seeing in these what we cannot or will not see in ourselves. If we go so far as to call this intuition, we are definitely in deep water!

RELEASING THE PAST

Sometimes we get stuck on a particular feeling and can't get through it. We relive our trauma time and again, thinking that somehow we'll find a way to make the pain subside. But focusing on the past this way tells us *nothing* about what we need to do now, or next. Often we hide behind these attachments, using them to protect us from having to change and move on.

If you find yourself struggling with something of this

sort, here are a few things to try. First, in privacy and quietude, relive the past once more, only this time *make it the way you wish it had been.* Sometimes this alone will clarify changes you need to make, the hidden meaning for you personally in what transpired.

Commonly, these are situations where we've given up our power and have thus experienced great loss. It is therefore necessary to mourn this loss, to grieve and forgive ourselves in order to move forward. Tremendous healing and release await when we surrender to this process.

Diane Mariechild likens this process of letting go to that of being washed by "cleansing rains." In her meditation/visualization of the same name, she evokes a state of tension with the image of clouds massing overhead, and then of release as the rains "come trickling."[6] As we imagine the rains washing over us at last and down to the earth beneath, we feel a part of nature, cleansed of our woes and alienation. "Feel the comfort," she invites, "that comes from releasing long-held emotions; feel the freedom."

SHIFTING ATTENTION

I first became familiar with the practice of shifting attention from an agitated to relaxed emotional state through the process of giving birth. But it works just as well in a variety of everyday situations.

For example, imagine yourself in a horrendous traffic

jam, already late for an appointment, no car phone and nothing on the radio. It is hot, your car is beginning to over-heat, and the person behind you is honking incessantly. Or, imagine yourself waiting for your lover to come home from a meeting—things have been tense between you lately, and he's nearly an hour late.

We typically respond to such scenarios by becoming emotionally disturbed and reactive. There is another choice, however; the neat little trick of shifting attention to a more relaxed, and thus transcendent state.

If this strikes you as being act of cowardice, that's un-derstandable. We have more than a little tough-it-out, fight-to-the-death imprinting in this regard. But there is a major difference (and an important one) between *giving in*, and *giv-ing up*. Giving in can so expand the parameters of our situ-ation that stress just dissipates; at the same time, our per-spective shifts from irksome particulars to the overview. Giving up, on the other hand, connotes denial of feelings, closing down.

Let's look more closely at the example found in giving birth. There is a turning point fairly early when contractions become significantly stronger, and many women scramble desperately through their repertoire of techniques for some-thing to put them in control. If they give in to the process, go *right through* the sensation and out the other side, it usu-ally becomes easier to bear. But if they try to escape or plain give up, it becomes much more difficult.

Sheila Kitzinger, authority on childbirth preparation, was one of the first to realize the importance of emotional release in achieving physical relaxation. It's one thing to let go when you're cool, calm and collected; quite another when feeling angry, frustrated or threatened.

Try this technique from her book, *The Experience of Childbirth*, which she terms "noticing tension."

> The next time you are in an upsetting situation, take careful note of your physical reactions. Later, when relaxed and quiet, recreate the situation in your mind and feel the tension fully again. Then take a break, relax completely and see if you can *stay relaxed* as you recreate the situation once more.

Ideally, one can learn to meet stressful situations with an attitude of surrender, much as one tries to greet labor contractions with complete release. Though far from being easy, this is definitely a way of moving to a more synchronous, intuitive state.

Helen Palmer, intuition trainer and author of *The Enneagram*, sees shifting attention as a most powerful trigger of intuition, particularly in situations where one is mortally afraid. Her prime example is the "lion in the middle of the road" phenomenon, corroborating the role of adrenaline. In this context, emotional intensity *serves as a springboard* for intuitive awareness! Harking back to what was said earlier about "needing to have a charge to make it work," Ms. Palmer defines the intuitive moment as the interaction of attention with a high degree of psychic arousal. The trick, she says, is "holding attention steady in the midst of what scares you the most." Thus you may be excruciatingly aware of external goings-on and still manage to shift to an internal source of knowing, as though seeing with inner eyes.

Go ahead and practice this by using the latter part of Kitzinger's exercise, i.e., recreate some frightening situation you've experienced, feel the fear and then shift your attention to a neutral space, or if you will, "from fear to field." You will probably experience a rush of energy as you let go—a taste of theta-like coherence.

I have several examples of how this has worked for me in crisis. Should a life-threatening situation suddenly develop at a birth I'm assisting, I've learned to open my body, yield physically to my fear in order to act appropriately. I have been amazed to find my hands performing complicated maneuvers virtually unknown to me, in order to free a stuck baby or control a hemorrhage. There were other theta-like qualities in these experiences—a sense that time hung suspended, tremendous energy passing through me, and the feeling of being grabbed and guided by a greater force of intelligence.

Another example (though less profound) sometimes occurs when I feel blocked at writing. I realize I'm afraid I don't know enough, or have nothing worthwhile to say. If I open my mind by shifting from fear's edge to my inside story, the words come pouring out again.

Along these lines, Palmer speaks of embracing one's "neurotic style" or eccentric way of being as key to opening the intuitive gate. Perhaps the intuitive process is a lot more subjective than we think, if personal fears and/or neuroses are such profound triggers!

Being Authentic

One of the pitfalls in any effort to expand consciousness is that one might become so enamored with enlightenment as to completely lose one's individuality. Perhaps you've known people like this; they are undeniably high-energy but rather one-track, and you get the distinct impression that "the lights are on but nobody's home."

Well, when it comes to utilizing intuition one must have a voice, a well-honed and responsible means of expression. This is where authenticity comes in.

You may have noticed in the last few exercises the presence of a subtly objective side of yourself, a part of you that simply observes all the thoughts, images and feelings flowing through. This aspect is rather paradoxical, isn't it—decidedly individual and yet surprisingly universal.

Learning to stay connected to this core element of your being, checking in with it, listening to it and trusting it, is critical to intuitive function. It is through this observer aspect that the intuitive voice speaks!

Larry Ramirez, Native American authority on transpersonal states, gives an example of tribal lore that illustrates the importance of keeping one's essential self. When taking up the hunt, he cautions, "learn the habits and ways of the animal, walk with the animal until you get what you need, but never forget that you're not that animal!" In other words, you protect what is valuable to you (your life) by guarding and cherishing it.

How many of us cherish ourselves on anything resembling a regular basis? More often, we drop everything at the whims of those around us. Angie Arrien gives five universal reasons why we abandon ourselves:

1) for someone else's love

2) for someone else's acceptance

3) for peace

4) for balance

5) for harmony[7]

All this is fairly typical behavior for women, conditioned as we are to serve and consider the needs of others first. And we are therefore doubly oppressed by losing what is most dear to us *and* most functional in interacting with those we care about.

Whenever the true self is abandoned, a false persona grows. On the other hand, as Gertrude Stein reminds us, "No one real is boring." We must learn to listen first and foremost to the inner voice, at the risk of displeasing others, at the risk of change or upheaval. To quote Arrien once more, " 'No' is a complete sentence." We are victims in any area where we cannot say this simply and clearly.

One of the most profound practices for developing authenticity is to strive for consistency in thought, word and deed. This means being honest, of course, but it also involves what a friend of mine terms "showing up." We show up when we let what's inside of us be expressed, when there is no separation between our inner and outer selves. Showing up may mean verbalizing or it may mean being quietly receptive, so long as our energy is running and not held back. The more we listen to and respect what the inner voice has to tell us, the more spontaneous and appropriate will be our actions, although there may be some difficulties at first in ridding ourselves of old constructs in work and relationships.

We can find guidance and support for this via the archetype of the warrior (though generally considered a masculine figure, remember the female Amazonians and soldiers of Crete). It was probably Carlos Castaneda who best translated the mythical qualities of the warrior into everyday attributes, focusing particularly on that of *impeccability*. This is nearly a synonym for consistency, except that it connotes even greater vigilance and precision. Consider that the warrior's life hangs constantly in the balance, thus total attention is necessary at every moment.

And what does the warrior-as-archetype battle? Any limitations and constrictions of the authentic self! Says Mariechild:

> The warrior . . . is animated by inner poise and fearlessness . . . (her) power is the power of the will, a clear and strong intention that is aligned with the energy of the universe.[8]

This unstinting awareness of one's place in life develops yet another critical attribute, that of *discernment*. We all know truth is relative, that we inevitably affect and alter "facts" though personal filtering systems. Our discernment of *just how this is so* is key to being able to differentiate intuition from our fears, projections, hopes, desires and so forth.

In order to speak with fully authentic voices, constructivist women find they must "jump outside the frames and systems authorities provide and create their own . . ."[9] *The cornerstones of these personal superstructures are our intentions.* If they are core, clear and heartfelt, whatever we build upon them will have purpose and integrity.

How to become conscious of your true intentions? Begin by observing the patterns of your life, the themes that repeat themselves again and again. Note the experiences that keep recurring, lessons you never seem to learn. Herein lie the keys to your destiny. I'm reminded of an old Native American chant, "We are the weaver, we are the web," which shows how we become what we believe.

Make it a habit to chart progress on your intentions, at least once a week. Identifying and fulfilling a mission that is central to your purpose in life does more for your authenticity than almost anything else!

Meeting Your Intuitive Self

Now, a chance to make contact with your intuitive side by allowing your imagination to bring it to life. Do this exercise when you are certain not to be interrupted.

Choose a place and position relaxing to you.
Then close your eyes, and sense fully the room

around you. Now imagine getting up and walking outside . . . be aware of your movements, feel as though you are actually doing this.

Now picture yourself in a place especially beautiful or somehow sacred to you, a place you've been before or one that springs from your imagination. Bring yourself fully into this environment, feel your body present as before. your motions of settling down.

And now, emerging from the scene comes an aspect of your knowingness, your wise, intuitive self. She may appear as a different person, or as a slightly altered double of you—either is fine. Feel yourself fully present again, and when you are ready, ask your intuitive self if she has anything to tell you. You might want to take her hand, feel the connection between you.

When you are ready, say farewell and watch her depart. Let the scene fade, and bring yourself back to the place outside where you began. Then come back into the room again, and open your eyes.

Now, take a moment to contemplate the nature and demeanor of your intuitive self. Had she qualities you've thought missing (or deeply buried) in you? And her words—did she speak things you know in you heart to be true?

Embodying your intuition is really just a way of bringing your deepest, most authentic aspect to the surface. Know and love this part of yourself; let it speak to you and let it out with others! Align yourself with it, and your intuition will flow freely.

1. Belenky, *et al.*, *Women's Ways of Knowing* (New York: Basic Books, 1986).

2. *Ibid.*

3. Vaughan, Frances, *Awakening Intuition* (New York: Anchor Books, 1979).

4. Belenky, *et al.*, *op. cit.*

5. Ruddick, Sara, "Maternal Thinking," *Feminist Studies*, 6, (1980).

6. Mariechild, Diane, *The Inner Dance* (Freedom, CA: Crossing Press, 1987).

7. Arrien, Angeles, notes from workshop, "Ways of Seeing: Cross-Cultural Aspects of Intuition," (San Francisco, 1988).

8. Mariechild, *op. cit.*

9. Belenky, *et al.*, *op. cit.*

CHAPTER 4

Letting Intuition Work for You

This chapter will provide you ways to put intuition to work in your life, in a variety of professional and personal situations. But first, one of the most important questions of all: *how do we recognize intuition?* We know what it is and where it resides, but how can we know for sure when it comes to us?

Goldberg observes that intuition is often preceded by a herald-of-sorts, subtly announcing its arrival. This is usually felt as a *shift in consciousness*, a sense of waking up and becoming more alert, more finely-tuned. Learning to acknowledge this intimation of intuition is key to being able to make the most of it.

The first hint of intuition may feel like little more than

a flash in the corner of your mind, a shadow upon your awareness. The most important thing at this point is to remain unattached, steady in watchful waiting. This is more easily accomplished by shifting to a neutral state, or by focusing on your body, letting the message manifest within you. In other words, bear witness, open up and allow it to run its course.

At some point the meaning may emerge, in the form of a word, emotional feel or visual image. Remain in neutral until you sense some resolution or spontaneous completion. Then, after a bit of a breather, you can review and make note of what happened.

It may be helpful to keep a journal of these episodes, leaving blank space at the end of each to later record how things panned out. Sometimes it may be difficult to say, particularly if you have used intuition to make some decision and there is no way of knowing what would have happened otherwise. In this case, note how acting on your hunch *made you feel*. In general, following your inner feelings should lead to a sense of well-being, increased energy and power. Conversely, when you negate or set aside intuition you will probably experience fatigue, stress, emotional or physical discomfort. Harking back to the importance of authenticity, most of us eventually learn (albeit by trial and error) that our choices in life are really rather limited; we must do *what's right for us* or nothing turns out well!

Specific inclusions in your journal should include the date and time, perhaps the point in your cycle, the basic message and its source (yourself, another person, something you read or heard, etc.). You might note what you were doing immediately prior to the intuition and how it felt to you, both during and after. It is especially useful to describe *why* you chose to accept the message, or reject it as the case may be.

Different Intuitive Styles

If you pay close attention you may also notice that you tend to receive messages either physically, emotionally or mentally. These are merely different modalities, none superior or inferior to the other.

Physical intuition is generally felt as an opening or rushing sensation in a particular body center, most commonly in the heart or the gut. It may simply be a signal that messages are about to arrive on other levels (emotional, mental) or may be sufficient unto itself. It should not, however, be confused with the gripping or tightening sensations characteristic of emotional states like fear or anxiety; these are, by my definition, *instinctive* responses, though the two may nearly coincide.

Physical intuition may also be accessed and utilized deliberately. I learned this in assisting births; when labor became stalled or obstructed, I often found that by making physical contact with the mother (holding her shoulders or her feet) and opening myself fully, *I could feel in my own body* where she was tense or holding back. Then, by running energy through us both, I could help her let go and make progress again. I've already mentioned several times my intuition in birth crises, the profound sense of being guided in action. Another example of physical intuition occurs in lovemaking—those times when your lover seems to know exactly where and how you want to be touched, or when the two of you open to this knowingness together and feel yourselves as one. And it's definitely at play in active sports, when timing is perfect or performance inspired. Running energy is key to all of these, as is surrender to the process.

Emotional intuition is tricky; we've seen already how fear or desire can masquerade as the real thing. The difference is subtle; it regards our degree of attachment. In essence, feelings of attraction or aversion, that a particular action is desirable or to be avoided, must have *no apparent justification or reward* to qualify as intuitions.

The phenomenon of love at first sight, particularly when the subject seems rather unlikely, may be an example of emotional intuition. So may be the feeling to travel on a whim, despite major logistical difficulties. Simply being aware of our feelings and willing to follow them all the way through can trigger emotionally-based intuitions.

Vaughan notes that "expanding awareness of the emotional level of intuition is often associated with an increase in synchronicity." For example, you suddenly feel like calling someone up and the first thing you hear is, "I was just thinking about you." Frequently, the content or quality of these communications is especially significant.

You might also sense times to hold back from certain activities in spite of strong desires otherwise—these are the letters you tear up, the phone calls you never complete. The trouble is that you may feel as though you're giving up when you're only giving in, that your identity is on the line when in fact it's still intact. Such reactions are cues to shift to neutral and let your observer aspect size up the situation more objectively.

Mental intuitions are those sudden apprehensions of overall pattern wherein solutions to problems are magically revealed. Very often these appear as images of diagrams or models that tie everything together. This is the "Eureka" phenomenon, already discussed at length.

On the other hand, mental intuition can also be used to *formulate theories or hypotheses*, as opposed to discerning specific solutions. Intuitive conceptualization of a writing, painting or music project falls into this category, as may creative organizational development. The key to using this intuitive mode lies in finding a way to release concentration, relinquish control, long enough to experience a more comprehensive state of awareness.

The Role of Dreams

What about the images and configurations we meet in our dreams? Can these be interpreted as intuitions, trusted as such?

Essentially, dreams formulate and express what we already know intuitively. But the images may be so outrageous and complex as to defy simple interpretation. Dream content may be haunting, but without some means of making sense, generally remains enigmatic.

Experts in the field agree that a deductive or conclusive approach to dream interpretation must be avoided, noting the highly subjective and essentially fluid relationship of dreamer to dream. Perhaps the most well-known authority on the subject, Carl Jung, said outright, " . . . there is no definite or straight-forward interpretation of any dream,"[1] and maintained that determination of meaning should *always* be left to the individual. Nevertheless, he firmly believed that dreams serve to create psychic balance by compensating for personality quirks and deficiencies. I think they present a unique opportunity to discern one's psychological underpinnings (central issues in development, obstacles and threats to authenticity), thus facilitating work on one's intuitive aspect.

What about those chilling psychic dreams, precognitions that later turn out to be true? Numerous studies have shown that ESP phenomena commonly occur in the dream state, particularly premonitions of things to come.[2] Whatever the standard register of brain waves in dream sleep, it seems logical that a shift to theta would be easier to accomplish without the distractions and demands of waking consciousness. Thus visions of the future seem remarkably likely.

I recently spoke to a woman who had for many years been troubled by pre-cognitive dreams of disasters, only to find these events in the headlines or hear them on the morning news. She was so upset by these uncontrollable visions that for a long time she told no one, and suffered in silence. It was only when her dreams shifted to the past, providing visions of times and places in which she felt herself *personally* involved, that she got up the courage to see a therapist for assistance.

Of course, one can never know if a dream is pre-cognitive until after the fact, and it may be the facts are never known. True, these dreams tend to have an unusually vivid, emotionally-charged intensity, but so can nightmares or recurrent dreams. The best bet is to use a journal once again, keeping track of hits and misses.

Any dream that is recurrent or deeply disturbing to us personally gives ground for work on ourselves, and a perfect opportunity to bring the warrior-aspect to the fore. If we so choose, we can deliberately recreate and relive these terrifying dreams while in a meditative state and *give them any ending we desire!* Rather than running away in fear, or letting ourselves be swallowed up by some force of opposition, we can at the critical moment stand firm, bring the authentic self forward and do or say what we *really want*. This is a great way to get at the grit of who we are.

There is yet another way that dreams can facilitate intuition. In terms of problem-solving, I've found that if I formulate my question or concern right before I go to sleep, holding it gently as I drift off, I'll often wake with new ideas or the answer I need. Hence the advice to "sleep on it" may be truly efficacious. It is critical, however, to have pen and paper by the bed since these insights fade rapidly after the first waking moments. This includes the 4 AM insight—don't think it will hold until morning!

Invoking Intuition

In general, the intuitive process works one of two ways. We can allow a free-flow of thoughts and images to suggest a course of action, then investigate this with the aid of the rational mind. Or we can consider all the possibilities on a rational level, gather all the facts, then shift to a receptive state for intuitive guidance and input. Occasionally, the two combine in an eclectic fashion when we find ourselves alternating back and forth.

Now let's take a look at some specific situations in which we might wish to use intuition: creative work, problem-solving, decision-making and interpersonal relations. We'll see which of the above approaches works best for each of these, along with techniques to facilitate.

INTUITION AND CREATIVITY

When seeking to invoke the muse, there are definite ways to set the stage. The basic approach would be free-flow, taking a soft, open focus rather than fixing on specific creative desires or intentions.

One of the best ways to accomplish this is by *deliberately exposing yourself to new impressions*, getting out and about in some unfamiliar part of town, speaking to people "not your type" or reading books out of your usual area of interest. Remember how women making the transition from perceived to constructed knowing often felt the need to take time off, to do something they had never done before? In a sense, this is a play for overload, letting beta intensity shift awareness to one's underlying creative distillations.

A friend of mine terms this process "vagabonding" and points out that it is possible both on the road and in the arm-chair. Goldberg terms these venturings "absorption sessions." Whichever we choose, the function is to diffuse our attention so greatly that we lose self-consciousness, at which point the intuitive voice may be heard. And too, the intuitive mind makes use of these varied impressions in forming analogies and pulling together information for future use.

Physical activities for stimulating creativity include all the alpha-inducers like dancing, running, exercise and so forth. Relaxation practices, meditation and guided imagery also work. Emotional clearing may be key. And mental activities that deal with symbology, such as reading poetry or doing tarot, are especially evocative. So is reading philosophy, science fiction—anything that introduces some element of surprise will do!

Though we've already established that the split-brain theory goes only so far, we'd not be complete on this subject without a look at the work of Betty Edwards, author of *Drawing on the Right Side of the Brain*. She advocates a technique for working on creative projects that involves deliberate shifting from one hemisphere to the other. For example, one formulates a utilitarian image, outline or blueprint with rational capacity (left brain), then a more fanciful, poetic version with intuitive capacity (right brain). By learning the unique modalities of each state of mind, one can henceforth shift the project back and forth at will—left for details, right for inspiration. This is the eclectic approach in action, by which one not only invokes the muse but gives form to whatever she has to say. I'm certain many artists know this process intimately, sometimes delighting in it and other times finding it the height of schizophrenia. But such is the nature of human consciousness and the machine we call the brain.

INTUITIVE PROBLEM-SOLVING

Problem-solving, as I use the term here, refers to an open-ended search for an unknown solution. Decision-making is different, involving a choice between known alternatives (we'll take this up in the next section).

Nel Noddings, author of *Awakening the Inner Eye: Intuition in Education*, defines intuition in the realm of problem-solving as "the product of tension between subjective certainty and objective uncertainty." This requires an ability to tolerate ambiguity, to trust oneself implicitly in the search for understanding. Constructivist women are particularly good at this, wanting to avoid what they consider a shortcoming in many men, i.e., the tendency to compartmentalize or otherwise break the ties that bind things together.[3] It is the nature of women to think inclusively anyway, to be able to hold several perspectives at once, to work on numerous projects all at the same time. Undoubtedly this is due in part to the lessons of childbearing and child rearing. Yet few of us see these abilities as assets; we persist in thinking ourselves disorganized. The bottom line is found in the popular riddle, "What does the work of five men?" Answer: "One woman." Sexist though it is, it's one of my favorites!

This correlates to a classic method of problem-solving which is also highly intuitive, that of brainstorming, or bringing up as many thoughts and ideas on a subject as possible. None should be considered too bizarre, crazy or irrelevant; all can serve to stimulate the creative process through free association. The more ideas, the better! In fact, it is often wise to commit to generating ideas for a full fifteen or twenty minutes, in order to avoid premature closure should an appealing solution arise. Likely candidates can then be subjected to hard scrutiny and whittled down, or brainstormed all over again.

Other techniques for intuitive problem-solving include those that involve making an analogy of some sort to create a change in perspective.[4] For example, Einstein used direct analogy to envision himself riding a beam of light, literally projecting himself into his quest for understanding. When seeking a solution to a less abstract and more personal problem, one might similarly immerse oneself totally in the issue, pulling out all rational stops in the search for inner configurations and meaning.

Symbolic analogy is especially good for those with a strong propensity to visualization. For example, say you want to make some change in your stress-ridden life by slowing down, but are not yet certain how to begin. Using guided imagery to envision a rose, you might let but a single petal open daily, each bearing some hint not only of *what* to do but *how* to go about it. Or, say you are working on a creative project and are stumped for a conclusion. By envisioning the project as an elaborate meal cooked just to perfection, you might see clues in the arrangement of dishes, their overall pattern of appearance that indicates the final turn to take.

Yet another approach involves deliberately viewing situations in reverse. For example, say you've found out that your lover has betrayed you, and you're utterly devastated. Turn it around and imagine yourself as the betrayer, exploring all the feelings, good and bad. This may help you find an appropriate response, beyond getting locked in reaction. On a more tangible level, say you are struggling with financial worries. Imagine yourself with money to burn, and carefully observe your demeanor. There may be something in how you carry yourself, how you walk, dress, etc., that suggests an attitude more conducive to prosperity, or tells of changes you need to make in your life. This is what Robert Gerard, metaphysical author and psychotherapist to the rich and famous, calls "extracting the constructive essence from the poles of opposition."[5]

These suggestions depend on the element of detachment, stepping back and observing how your actions and behavior impact on your problem. In so doing, you may discover a deeper strata of feeling heretofore unrecognized yet sneaking out in body language, tone of voice or general appearance. Above all, try to discern what your authentic self already knows about the situation and is trying to communicate. By remaining in your observer aspect and not pushing for a solution, a vivid understanding of what it's all about and why you're a part of it may suddenly emerge.

It's noteworthy that these methods of analogy are but practical applications of the techniques presented in Chapter Three: immersion through personal analogy is the essence of meditation; working with symbology evokes one's authenticity; viewing situations in reverse stimulates emotional clearing and detachment. One thing these all have in common is that they *provide a way to get beyond hard data.* This is critical, since hard data represent only what is already known, i.e., in the past. In order to find a comprehensive solution we must have a look at the future. This is where soft data, gleaned intuitively through the methods described above, may foretell what is to come. In fact, these techniques draw directly on the universal field, that time-free zone wherein all information is readily accessible.

Here is a meditation, adapted from many sources, that illustrates this perfectly.

> Choose a private place in which to relax, where you'll not be disturbed for a while. Pose whatever problem is troubling you, and be one with it, let it fill you completely.
>
> Now imagine yourself at some water's edge; there is a small boat waiting for you. Once inside, you settle in comfortably and drift slowly from shore. Gently the waves lap at the boat, and you relax, knowing the boat will take you exactly where you need to go.

Gradually the sky darkens, and soon you enter a cave and begin moving through an underground passage. It is very dark, but you are not afraid. Then off in the distance there is light, and you emerge in an immense subterranean cavern. You float slowly to the far shore, where your boat finally comes to rest.

You climb out and sit on some nearby rocks, watching tiny waves break at the shore's edge. Suddenly, someone comes from behind and taps you on the shoulder, speaking some message, or passing a vision to your mind. Just accept this completely, and don't try to analyze now.

After a while, you get back in your boat and are swiftly transported back to the shore where you began. Now contemplate the meaning of what you experienced.

INTUITIVE DECISION-MAKING

Weston Agor, author of the book *Intuitive Management*, did a fascinating study on the use of intuition by top-level executives for various kinds of decision-making. Of some 2,000 participants, upper-level managers in every organization scored higher than lower or mid-level managers in their ability to let intuition guide major decisions. In describing the characteristics of this group, Agor found them to be "particularly adept at generating new ideas and providing ingenious solutions to old problems; usually they function best in rapidly changing environments or crisis settings." This strikes me as a remarkably apt description of a good mother, although it might also apply to a resourceful teacher in an inner-city school, a top-notch hot-line therapist or an expert in emergency care.

At any rate, Agor did a follow-up study on the top 10% of those surveyed, in order to obtain more in-depth information. From this group of 200, here is a list of conditions considered optimal for intuitive decision-making:

1) a high level of uncertainty exists;

2) little previous precedent exists;

3) facts don't clearly point the way to go;

4) analytical data are of little use;

5) several plausible alternative solutions exist to choose from, with good arguments for each;

6) time is limited and there is pressure to come up with the right decision.[6]

Such conditions might cause the less adventuresome to freeze in fear, or to put decision-making on hold indefinitely. Attitude makes all the difference; it's the willingness to *play* with alternatives, *entertain* notions or *toy* with options that is crucial to success.

But before we can expect intuition to work effectively in this mode, we must make sure we have *posed the right question*. Sounds a bit silly and self-evident, doesn't it? Yet unless we create the appropriate context, no satisfactory answer can possibly be found.

Adair believes that when the question is clear, it acts as a flashlight, illuminating "the particular spot in the amorphous collective unconscious where the answer resides." This may mean paring a general question down to some specific concern, or revamping it all together. For example, say you are trying to decide whether to quit your job for compelling creative endeavors, or maintain the status quo long enough to qualify for paid vacation or temporary leave. It would be easy to go back and forth on this indefinitely. But consider a series of exploratory questions, like: "Why do I want to keep my job, anyway?"; "Is it only for the money, or is there something personally gratifying about my work?"; "Do I *really* want one or the other, or perhaps a little of both?" Hence evolves a question nearer the heart of the matter: "How can I combine the best of my work with my creative pursuits?" This question is more easily answered because it has ceased to be either/or, and may thus respond better to the open-ended, problem-solving modality.

Another example of getting to the question might begin with the dilemma of whether to go on a speaking tour or stay home to cultivate a new love interest. Here the line of questioning might run: "Is there anything I can do to consolidate this new relationship so I can be away and still feel secure?"; "What if I put off my engagements for another six months, would that work for me professionally?"; "Which is really more important to me *right now*, my job or my love-life?" Now we're at the core issue, I'd say, although either choice is merely a take-off point for additional decision-making.

Sometimes we discover the appropriate question not by a process of whittling down, but of expansion. For example, say you're trying to decide whether to buy a house near the city where property values are highest, or way out in the suburbs where values are lower but life more relaxed. Here the question may not pertain to dollars and cents at all, but to an underlying desire for change in lifestyle. A more appropriate question might be: "Why consider the suburbs at all—what is it about living there that appeals to me?"

In summary, we severely limit intuition's ability to guide us if we oversimplify issues, fail to look beyond the obvious parameters of our question or remain blind to our presumptions. This is why seeking a fresh angle on the subject is such a help. It is also important to remember that problems seldom exist in isolation, but clustered within a larger configuration. Thus meditative techniques to tune us to the bigger picture may also be crucial.

Sometimes dilemmas remain stubbornly either/or; there seems no way to redefine them. In this case try projecting yourself *several years hence*, first with one option, then the other. Notice the ambience, the images and feelings that emerge. This may assist you in making a decision.

Whenever we get locked in a struggle to decide, it's likely to be because we fear making the wrong choice. But there really is *no such thing as a right or wrong decision*, since either way will inevitably lead to turns both pleasing and disappointing. Besides, it is terribly disruptive of one's authenticity to go back and agonize repeatedly, "If only I had . . ." How in the world can we ever account for all possible variables—what a set-up for frustration and defeat! We may not always be happy with our choices, but this is no cause to invalidate them.

Still, it is important to remember that we *are accountable* for what we do. Whatever we choose, we must take responsibility. It may be tempting from time to time to say, "Intuition made me do it," but this can lead to the most blatant fanaticism unless we deliberately expose our intuitive promptings to both rational and ethical consideration.

It helps to reevaluate our belief systems periodically to see how we frame our choices, particularly if we seem faced with the same decision again and again. Whether the result of personal history or cultural conditioning, it's useful to trace back fundamental beliefs and choose consciously to either keep or discard them. The empowering thing about this process is that you may develop a narrative sense of yourself, both backwards and forwards in time.

You might also get in touch with your ancestry, particularly your female line. You can make this the subject of a meditation if you like, invoking your grandmother, great-grandmother, etc. to come and stand behind you. This will heighten your awareness of your heritage, and may clarify the unique role you play in the evolution of your lineage.

One more thing: sometimes it's best to let a decision rest if no answer seems to be forthcoming. The best way to accomplish this is via the creative mode, deliberately seeking new impressions, greater exposure to the world around you. This may freshen your perspective sufficiently to make another go of it.

INTERPERSONAL INTUITION

The use of intuition to assist, or somehow discern the truth about another is fraught with danger. Not that it can't be done, but one must always follow the rule: *only with consent.* Even with the best intentions—to help someone who is suffering or in crisis—there is always the risk of disrupting some delicate balance beyond our immediate comprehension, thus incurring some indebtedness or entanglement much more complex than we ever expected. It's an ethical issue, really, one that arises whenever we involve ourselves or otherwise meddle in the affairs of others. It is noteworthy that many psychics follow this rule religiously, refusing to give information on spouses, children, etc. without their express permission.

One simple way to use intuition to illuminate personal relations is through *shared* intuitive processes. Women often do this in simple conversation, following the basic tenets of brainstorming and alternately embracing the roles of observer and passionate knower. This kind of communication, called "real talk" by constructivist women, is rare among men.[7] Men tend to hold forth rather than share ideas, to report experience perhaps, but without the desire to arrive at new understanding. "Real talk" implies the agreement to create an optimal setting for those "half-baked," emerging ideas to grow. This may involve doubting or questioning one another's notions from time to time; not in an adversarial way but in a spirit of *faith and support*.

What if you desire intuitive communication with someone clearly unreceptive or unwilling—your boss, perhaps, or your husband? Holding to the aforementioned rule, you can hardly engage them against their will or knowledge. About your only recourse is to *reframe your concern so the focus is on you*. For example, say you are experiencing stresses in the household regarding domestic chores, but every time you broach the subject it turns into a battle. You'd love to explore the possibilities creatively and find a mutually satisfying solution, but your partner is too threatened or otherwise unable to participate. So brainstorm your *own* solutions, steps *you* can take to create the order you need and/or ways to meet the difficulty with your partner by really "showing up." Even when "real talk" sessions *are* possible, most interpersonal problems still require a good bit of work you must do on your own.

Now let's look once more at the problem of projection. We've discussed already how important it is to own one's feelings, so as not to imagine others as cause or source. Ordinarily, we rely on our external perceptions to discern truths regarding those around us. In an intuitive mode, however, we rely more on the inner observer to interpret our relationship to the outer world. Sometimes, in moments of great love or crisis, it may happen that there is a *direct transfer* of information from the outer world, or object of our concentration, to the inner observer. This peak experience of merging is a gift, wonderful, exhilarating. It can also intoxicate or overwhelm our judgment unless we're able to *tell the difference* between these transpersonal impressions and our own projections.[8]

This is certainly one of the great challenges of any intimate relationship, especially in the early stages. If you've ever gotten "lost in love," you know the incredible confusion and grief this can bring. Here we have a clear example of why relentless self-awareness is essential for responsible intuitive communication.

We can sum up all the recommendations of the previous sections with the following statement by Gerard, "The higher the motivation, the higher the intuition." You can use intuition to decide whether or not to go shopping, or to determine your true role in society; it's up to you. Intuition works best and takes us farthest when our purpose is in harmony with the greater good, when we observe respect for the powers-that-be and seek to align ourselves with them. This may seem a lofty goal at first, but as you practice listening to your intuitive voice and responding with integrity you'll start feeling *so good*, so much a part of everything that anxieties about right and wrong, what others do or don't do will begin to subside. Before long, your life will have a rhythm and meaning all it's own, and using your intuition will be second-nature.

1. Jung, Carl, *Man and His Symbols* (New York: Doubleday, 1964).

2. Hasting, Arthur, "Dreams of Future Events: Precognitions and Perspectives," *Journal of the American Society of Psychosomatic Dentistry and Medicine* (1977).

3. Belenky, *et al.*, *Women's Ways of Knowing* (New York: Basic Books, 1986).

4. Goldstein, *et al.*, "Management on the Right Side of the Brain," *Personal Journal* (1985).

5. Gerard, Robert, notes from lecture, "Intuition and the Evolution of Consciousness—Integrating Personal and Transpersonal Intuition" (San Francisco, 1988).

6. Agor, Westin, "The Logic of Intuition: How Top Executives Make Important Decisions," *Organizational Dynamics* (1986).

7. Belenky, *et al.*, *op. cit.*

8. Palmer, Helen, notes from workshop, "Discrimination Between Projections and Accurate Intuitive Impressions" (San Francisco, 1988).

CHAPTER 5

Intuitive Self-Care & Renewal

As you have probably realized by now, even the most moving meditations and powerful techniques won't amount to much unless you find a way to tailor them to your situation. Thus you need some sort of plan, perhaps a routine of daily practices designed especially for you.

In Chapter Three, we explored the three major avenues for developing intuition: meditation, emotional clearing and authentic self-expression. Taken and used together, these create a healthy balance of inner-outer focus, personal and universal awareness. They are key to self-renewal, and form the foundation of daily practice. The *particular blend* of these, however, remains up to you.

You might begin with an equal-parts formula, allowing a certain amount of time for each. For example, plan on meditating every morning for half an hour or so. Remember how broad this category is; it includes almost anything relaxing and affirming to you personally, and may also include any of the meditations given in this book. Therefore your choice may vary from day to day, e.g., aerobic dance two days a week, guided visualization once or twice, inspirational music another day, and "running energy" whenever it feels right. The most important thing is to consciously identify these activities as meditations, since this will affect the manner in which you experience them.

Emotional clearing rather defies scheduling, but the practice of noticing feelings can be done on a routine basis. Releasing the past should be done whenever necessary; sometimes it may seem the work of choice for days on end. You might also try alternating the two: notice and release, notice and release. This will help you cultivate objectivity.

Shifting attention should be practiced whenever an appropriate situation presents itself, although basic technique can be maintained with Kitzinger's method of "noticing tension." A weekly review of overall efforts in emotional clearing will help you see how much time you've actually spent; it may be more than you think!

Work on authenticity can be quite deliberate and routine. The practice of checking in once or twice daily to assess your true state of being is not only basic, it's invaluable. Learning when to say "No" is obviously ongoing. Weekly assessment of progress on intentions is also a good idea.

Of course, you don't have to dedicate your life to developing intuition if you're not ready! Whatever you do, your efforts will accumulate with time. But do bear in mind that work in one area should be balanced with work in the others. Were you to throw yourself whole-heartedly into emotional clearing without the strengthening effect of authenticity practice or the release of meditation, you might become confused, overwhelmed or depressed. On the other hand, focusing on authenticity alone might render you a bit over-bearing, in need of the universal perspective of meditation and the sobering awareness of emotional work. It's fine to change the mix of these once and a while, as long as you keep an overview and don't go off the deep end.

This discussion of balance would be incomplete without a word about physical habits, and their impact on reaching heightened states of awareness. We need to differentiate genuinely rejuvenating practices from those used essentially as crutches.

I will mention yoga first because I think it works miraculously. It simultaneously accomplishes muscle toning, balanced stimulation of the master glands and psychological unification. It is definitely one of the most powerful tools for developing intuition; in fact, many who practice yoga experience this as an unexpected but much appreciated bonus.

On the other hand, relaxation practices that involve a forced attempt at letting go can be detrimental, raising issues of control and causing mental strain. Research has shown the practice of *tensing muscle groups before release* to be more physiologically sound, and thus more conducive to relaxation.[1]

This brings us to the practices which artificially relax

us, like the commonplace use of alcohol. Although some claim to feel intuitive during the initial phase of stimulation, drinking ultimately *dulls* our high-frequency sensitivities and linkage. This makes for a confusing state of psychic affairs, wherein hunches are readily waylaid by emotional reactions and should therefore not be trusted.

Stimulants like caffeine, sugar, chocolate, etc. may temporarily increase intuitive awareness by causing the release of adrenaline, but they also tax the adrenal glands and other body systems so that a reactive phase of confusion, fatigue and depression is not uncommon. Those who abuse these substances from time to time know the nearly immediate stabilizing effect of increased protein intake. Protein actually helps regulate adrenal function.[2] According to Rhea, it "slows transmission down so you can manage an incoming feeling and translate it before receiving another one."

These recommendations are basic common sense yet raise once again the issue of equilibrium. What one woman can get away with at a given point in time might lay another low for several days. Or as Marilyn Ferguson points out in her book, *The Aquarian Conspiracy*, the concept of health as a function of eating the right foods, taking the best supplements or doing the latest exercises is externally-based and therefore old-school. Superseding any routine of health-promoting practices is the need to *tune into your body*, to become aware of the physical voices speaking within you. A classic example is the voice of hunger, often violated by adults, yet remarkable trustworthy in little children (providing they're not yet corrupted by a taste for sugar or fast food).

Illness may occur when we fail to pay attention to our inner voices; not just the physical ones, but emotional ones as well. The term *dis-ease* tells all: one is out of sync with one's surroundings and oneself. The longer we ignore the message of disease in its minor manifestations (sporadic aches and pains, tension headaches), the more likely it is to progress to serious illness.

How does this relate to the subject of intuition? For one thing, interpreting the promptings of our bodies is highly intuitive work. And too, the practices involved in developing intuition are intense enough to cause physical side-effects for some. As Gawain points out, "In being true to yourself you will feel more alive, but you may also feel uncomfortable." By remapping your inner life you are giving yourself a major overhaul; it's only natural that your body might act out from time to time.

The tricky part in this is figuring out how to make yourself well. Sometimes you get a clear sense that a symptom is transitory, i.e., your stress is temporary, and the course you're on is about to take a turn for the better. For example, I woke with a sore throat the other morning, realized I needed to ask my husband for more help in order to complete this project, but knew since I was almost finished that there was no need to worry.

But if your symptoms are persistent or severe, you must get to the root cause. This may actually be the easy part; the challenge is finding a way to rid yourself of negative influences while at the same time examining the nature of your participation. Blaming external events won't help; neither will blaming yourself. A shifting-attention practice may be useful, if you first immerse yourself in the dilemma of your disease, then shift to your observer aspect for insight.

It may be, though, that your illness is serving you somehow, that you are actually getting more from being sick than you would from being well. If this rings a bell, here are a few questions for your consideration. What is the illness protecting you from? What is it providing you that is positive? And what would you do without it? You may find that you're not ready to be well, that you need more time to relax, to get into your feelings or reflect on concerns in your life. But perhaps you can find a way to have all these without also being sick!

Inglehart sums it up beautifully: "Anything we do to facilitate the flow of energy between different parts of ourselves and between ourselves and others is healing." Sometimes we simply need to retreat, and a much nicer way to do this than becoming ill is to take a vacation. In my most active years of midwifery practice, I quickly learned that the only way I could handle the intensity and stress of my work was with month-long breaks, preferably in a foreign country completely away from the phone. Rhea notes that those in the healing and helping professions often become oversensitized to their environment and desperately need some way to turn down the volume on their reception. Although we're taught to believe that the only way to get ahead is through the daily grind, considering what we've learned about quantum intuitive leaps in periods of relaxation, perhaps we've been duped!

Should it be that getting away is not enough, and major decisions and changes seem called for in your life, take heart. As difficult as these may be, you will gain in the end. Being in the wrong line of work, in a negative relationship or unhealthy living situation will only dampen your intuitive awareness. As Belenky, *et al.* make clear regarding those who manage to reach an integrated state of development, "Once a woman has a voice, she wants it to be heard."

This raises a most important point. If you begin to use the practices described in Chapter Four for bringing intuition into your life, you'd better have an appropriate outlet, or illness may be the least of your worries! It's a question of responsibility, a matter of spiritual frugality that *you only take what you can use*. The key to this, according to Arrien, is finding some way of "walking the mystical path with practical feet."

Here is where a deliberate process of removing old business from our lives may be essential. We create a vacuum and sure enough, something will rush in to fill it! Letting go of attachments and confronting the unknown is never easy, but it is one of life's greatest lessons (learned ultimately in death).

The emotions we feel in such a phase will not necessarily be pleasant. Fear may nearly paralyze us, anxiety scatter and distract our efforts. Anger is also common, anger at having to let go and change. But even rage, grief and depression may be *gateways to the spirit*, if we but own them and acknowledge their underlying meaning. Relying on intuition for inspiration and guidance while drawing on the authentic self for a vision of the future is probably the least destructive way to move through difficult or wrenching circumstances.

We have, I think, a metaphor in yet another major biological event in women's lives: the menopause. At first glance, this would seem a time of tremendous loss. But all those years of working through the heights and depths of the monthly cycle enable us, at last, to *transcend* it. The mythic, post-menopausal figure of the Old Crone represents wisdom that is refined, highly distilled, above hormonal fluctuation. She is in touch with the matrix beyond all voices, the point of stillness deep inside each one of us. Whenever we must endure extreme emotional pain, it is here we find our greatest solace.

It certainly helps to have some support, not only in times of trouble but for the general purpose of strengthening ourselves and affirming our intuitive abilities. Although fairly articulate, women in professional circles may be least free to discuss intuition because the "old guard" holds logic as king. No wonder these executive types may feel a constant need to "dress up a gut decision in data clothes."[3] Be that as it may, the issues raised by the use of intuition—power, ethics, personal health and balance—are so complex that help from others is practically a must.

Why not pull together a circle of friends for this purpose? Picture yourself in "real talk" with a few trusted confidants, gathering together once a month or so. You can reward each other for generating ideas, even if they end up being off the mark. You can help each other remember that the process is more important than the results. As Adair ob-

serves, "Circles are a powerful antidote to the isolation en-
demic to our society."

This raises an interesting question: to what extent is the
development of intuition a *social* issue? How might society
be impacted if we women became more intuitive?

I believe that well-developed intuitive ability in a responsible and caring person would most probably lead to a
state of *ethical attunement*. This is very different from the
externally-imposed sense of moral obligation engendered
by religious or professional codes. Such attunement is truly
love, not addictive or emotionally entangled but altruistic,
conscious. As we learn to love ourselves and empower the
authentic aspects of who we are, how can we help extending
the same to others? Once we know the truth of our existence, how inextricably linked we are to each other, our environment and the universe, responsibility springs naturally
from within.

Cultural belief systems come and go; concepts of right
and wrong may reverse themselves in as little as ten years'
time. That's why it is never enough to believe what everyone
else believes; we must know truth from the inside out.

But beyond this, we must act. Constructivist women are
known to be "seriously preoccupied with the moral or spiritual dimension of their lives . . . they strive to translate their
moral commitments into action . . . out of a feeling of responsibility to the larger community in which they live."[4]
One simple way to begin moving in this direction is to *let our
intuitive processes show*. If we allow others to see us as spontaneous, intensely curious, willing to chase notions up blind
alleys or entertain doubts without fear, we will inspire them

in their own quest for understanding. Particularly with our children it is crucial that we be honest, vulnerable and willing to admit mistakes. Likewise, we can foster their intuitive growth by allowing them a free range of interests, and by never making them afraid to guess, to dream.

As women, we can respect the cyclical nature of one another's energy and vitality, supporting and assisting so we all get breaks and opportunities when we need them most. We can use "connected" methods of evaluating one another's actions and behavior, rather than competitive ones. We can honor our biological turning points in menarche, birth, lactation and menopause with ritual and sharing. We can reclaim the wisdom of our past, and formulate a vision of the future.

Naturally, this will affect our social structure. It may lead to the development of new traditions, or an honoring of ancient ones. The impact of awakening intuition may reach farther still, creating a sense of international interconnectedness. This is, I would hope, the evolutionary path of our species, in which we women play a most significant and inspiring part.

---

1. Noble, Elizabeth, *Childbirth With Insight* (Boston: Houghton and Mifflin, 1983).

2. Rhea, Kathlyn, *Mind Sense* (Berkeley, CA: Celestial Arts, 1988).

3. Agor, Westin, "The Logic of Intuition: How Top Executives Make Important Decisions," *Organizational Dynamics* (1986).

4. Belenky, *et al.*, *Women's Ways of Knowing* (New York: Basic Books, 1986).

REFERENCES

Adair, Margo. *Working Inside Out*. Berkeley, CA: Wingbow Press, 1984.

Agor, Weston. "The Logic of Intuition: How Top Executives Make Important Decisions." *Organizational Dynamics*, 1986.

Agor, Weston. *Intuitive Management*. Englewood Cliffs, NJ: Prentice-Hall, 1984.

Arrien, Angeles. *The Tarot Handbook: Practical Applications of Ancient Visual Symbols*. Sonoma, CA: Arcus Publishing, 1987.

Assagioli, Robert. *Psychosynthesis*. New York: Hobbs Dohrman, 1965.

Belenky, Mary F., Clinchy, Blythe M., Goldberg, Nancy R., Tarule, Jill M. *Women's Ways of Knowing*. New York: Basic Books, 1986.

Bentov, Itzhak. *Stalking the Wild Pendulum: On the Mechanics of Consciousness*. New York: Dutton, 1977.

Capra, Fritjof. *The Tao of Physics*. Berkeley, CA: Shambhala, 1975.

d'Aquili, Eugene G. "The Neurobiological Basis of Myth and Concepts of Deity." *Zygon*. 1978.

Dellbeck, Michael C., and Bronson, Edward C. "Short-Term Longitudinal Effects of the Transcendental Meditation Technique on EEG Power and Coherence." *International Journal of Neuroscience.* 1981.

Dick-Read, Grantly. *Childbirth Without Fear.* New York: Harper & Row, 1959.

Edwards, Betty. *Drawing on the Right Side of the Brain.* Los Angeles: Tarcher, 1979.

Ferguson, Marilyn. *The Aquarian Conspiracy.* Los Angeles: Tarcher, 1980.

Freire, Paulo. *Pedagogy of the Oppressed.* New York: Seaview, 1971.

Garfield, Patricia. *Creative Dreaming.* New York: Ballantine, 1976.

Gawain, Shakti. *Living in the Light.* San Rafael, CA: Whatever Publishing, 1986.

Goldberg, Phillip. *The Intuitive Edge.* Los Angeles: Tarcher, 1983.

Goldstein, M., Scholthauer, D., Kleiner, B., "Management On the Right Side of the Brain." *Personal Journal,* 1985.

Gowan, John Curtis. *Development of the Psychedelic Individual.* New York: Creative Education Foundation, 1974.

Griffin, Susan. *Women and Nature.* New York: Harper & Row, 1978.

Grof, Stanislav. *Realms of the Human Unconscious.* New York: Viking Press, 1971.

Hastings, A. "Dreams of Future Events: Precognitions and Perspectives." *Journal of the American Society of Psychosomatic Dentistry & Medicine*, 1977.

Inglehart, Hallie Austen. *Woman Spirit*. San Francisco: Harper & Row, 1983.

Jung, Carl Gustav. *Man and His Symbols*. Garden City, NY: Doubleday, 1964.

Kitzinger, Sheila. *The Experience of Childbirth*, 5th ed. New York: Penguin, 1982.

Mariechild, Diane. *The Inner Dance*. Freedom, CA: Crossing Press, 1987.

McMillian, Carol. *Women, Reason and Nature*. Princeton, NJ: Princeton University Press, 1982.

Noble, Elizabeth. *Childbirth with Insight*. Boston: Houghton-Mifflin, 1983.

Noddings, Nel. *Awakening the Inner Eye: Intuition in Education*. New York: Teachers College Press, Columbia University, 1984.

Palmer, Helen. *The Enneagram*. New York: Harper & Row, 1988.

Peterson, Gayle. *Birthing Normally*. Berkeley, CA: Mind-Body Press, 1981.

Rhea, Kathlyn. *Mind Sense*. Berkeley, CA: Celestial Arts, 1988.

Rich, Adrienne. *On Lies, Secrets, and Silence: Selected Prose—1966-78*. New York: Norton, 1979.

Ruddick, Sara. "Maternal Thinking." *Feminist Studies*, 6, 1980. Reprinted in "Child Nurturance: Volume 1, Philosophy, Children and the Family." New York: Plenum Press, 1982.

Springer, Sally, and Deutsch, George. *Left Brain, Right Brain*. San Francisco: W. H. Freeman, 1981.

Stone, Merlin. *When God Was a Woman*. New York: The Dial Press, 1976.

Toben, Bob. *Space-Time and Beyond*. New York: Dutton, 1975.

Vaughan, Frances E. *Awakening Intuition*. Garden City, NY: Doubleday/Anchor, 1979.

Weil, Andre. *The Natural Mind*. Boston: Houghton Mifflin, 1972.

Westcott, Malcolm. *Toward a Contemporary Psychology of Intuition*. New York: Holt, Rinehart & Winston, 1968.

Wilber, Ken (ed.). *The Holographic Paradigm and Other Paradoxes: Exploring the Leading Edge of Science*. Berkeley, CA: Shambhala, 1982.

Zukav, Gary. *The Dancing Wu Li Masters*. New York: Morrow, 1979.

INDEX

Index

Inglehart, Hallie, 35–36, 80
"Insight", 2
Inspirational music, 76
Integration, 12
Intentions, becoming conscious
    of, 49
Interpersonal relations, 71–73
Intuition
    adrenaline and, 10, 12
    altered states and, 12
    biological inducements for,
        15–16, 24–32
    children and, 84
    creative work and, 60–62
    cultural inducements for, 16–
        18
    decision-making and, 66–71
    definitions of, 5–6
    developing, 2–3, 33–51
    disregarding, 10
    dreams and, 57–59
    embodying, 51
    emotional, 56–57
    interpersonal relations and,
        71–73
    invoking, 60–62
    mental, 57
    physical, 55–56
    problem-solving and, 62–73
    recognizing, 6–7, 53–74
    self-renewal and, 75–84
    social inducements for, 16–18
    as social issue, 83–84
    studies of, 12
    styles of, 55–57
    without context, 20

Intuitive Edge, The (Goldberg), 12
Intuitive Management (Agor), 66
Intuitive people, qualities of, 4

J
Jogging, 8
Journal
    to keep track of dreams, 59
    to keep track of emotions, 40
    to keep track of intuitions, 54–
        55
Jung, Carl, 58

K
Kitzinger, Sheila, 43–44, 45, 76
Knowing, stages of, 18–23. *See
    also specific stages of knowing*

L
Labor, 27–30, 55–56
Life-threatening struggles for
    survival, 9, 10
Limbic system, 12
Living in the Light (Gawain), 13
Love, 10
    emotional intuition and, 56
    ethical attunement as, 83
    interpersonal relations and, 73
    as meditation, 36
Lovemaking
    physical intuition and, 56
    theta waves and, 9

Index

Premenstrual Syndrome (PMS), 25
Premonitions, 58
Problems
    as meditation, 36
    mental intuition and, 57
Problem-solving, 15
    dreams and, 59
    intuition and, 62–73
Procedural knowing, 19, 20–21, 27
Professional circles, 82–83
Professional organizations, 21
Progesterone, 24, 26
Projection
    decision-making and, 69
    interpersonal relations and, 72–73
Prolactin, 30
Protein, 78
Psychedelic drugs, 9
Psychic dreams, 58
Purpose, 12
Puzzles, 36

Q

Qualities of Intuitive People (checklist), 4
Questions, 68–69

R

Rage, 16, 81
Ramirez, Larry, 46
Reading, 61
"Real talk", 71–72, 82–83

Received knowing, 19
Recurrent dreams, 59
Relaxation, 8, 61, 77–78, 80
Releasing the past, 41–42, 76
Retrocognition, 6, 59
Rhea, Kathlyn, 10, 35, 78, 80
Rhythmic activity, 8
Rich, Adrienne, 32
Ruddick, Sara, 41
Running
    creative work and, 61
    as meditation, 36
Running Energy (meditation technique), 37–38, 55–56, 76

S

Sacred intention, 10
Science fiction, 61
Self-defense, 18
Self-expression, 17
Self-help/support groups, 21
Self-renewal, 75–84
Sensationalism, 2
Sex, 9, 10, 56
Shifting attention, 42–45, 76, 80
Shock, 16
"Showing up", 47–48, 72
Sickness, 79–81
Silence, 19
Sleep cycles (maternal-infant), 30
Solutions, 57
Spirit, alignment of, 13
Split-brain theory, 11–12, 61–62
Sports, 56
Stages of knowing, 18–23

Index

Stein, Gertrude, 47
Stimulants, 78
Stress, 44
Struggles for survival, 9, 10
Subjective knowing, 19–21, 27
Sugar, 78
Superstition, 2, 20
Support groups, 21
Surrender, 44
Survival, struggles for, 9, 10
Swimming, 8
Symbolic analogy, 63–64
Symbology
    creative work and, 61
    problem-solving and, 65

T, U

Tantric lovemaking, 9
Tarot, 61
Tarule, Jill, 18, 31, 81
Telepathy, 6, 30
Tension headaches, 79
Thankfulness, 36
Theories, 57
Theta waves, 7, 9
    adrenaline and, 10
    alignment and, 12–13
    brain wave coherence and, 12
    children and, 10
    dreams and, 58
    expanded consciousness and,
      10–11
    labor and, 28
    pregnancy and, 27

Thoughts, recognizing, 6–7
Time/Space (contemplation), 39
*Toward a Contemporary Psychology
    of Intuition* (Wescott), 4
Travel, 56
Truth, 83

V

Vacations, 80
"Vagabonding", 61
Vaughan, Frances, 5, 39, 56
Viewing situations in reverse, 64,
    65
Vigilance, 48
Visualization, 63–64, 76

W, X

Weaving, 8
Wellness, 79–81
Westcott, Malcolm, 4
"Women's intuition", 2
Women's studies classes, 21
Women's Ways of Knowing (Belenky,
    et al.), 18
Work force, 17–18
Working Inside Out (Adair), 6
Writing
    as meditation, 36
    mental intuition and, 57

Y, Z

Yoga, 77